becoming
a
warrior

becoming a warrior

my journey to bring

a Wrinkle in Time
to the screen

a memoir

CATHERINE HAND

BOLD STORY PRESS

WASHINGTON, DC

Bold Story Press, Washington, DC 20016
www.boldstorypress.com

This book is a memoir and it reflects the author's
present recollections of experiences over time.

First edition published October 2022

Library of Congress Control Number: 2022904192

ISBN: 978-1-954805-33-0 (hard cover)
ISBN: 978-1-954805- 28-6 (paperback)
ISBN: 978-1-954805- 29-3 (e-book)

Text and cover design by KP Design
Cover illustration © MoVille/Shutterstock.com
Author photo © Tony Powell

Photos are from the author's personal
collection unless otherwise noted.
May 2, 1954 journal entry of Madeleine L'Engle used by
permission of Crosswicks, Ltd. All rights reserved.

Printed in the United States of America
10 9 8 7 6 5 4 3 2 1

For my mother and father
with an abundance of love and gratitude
and for Caitlin, Ben, and Meghan—
the lights of my life and the treasures of my heart

All through the universe it's being fought,
all through the cosmos, and my,
but it's a grand and exciting battle.

MADELEINE L'ENGLE

Contents

Introduction

*You know, there really is
such a thing as a tesseract.*

MADELEINE L'ENGLE

M ay 22, 2018, was an unusually hot day in Los Angeles. I was on the Walt Disney studio lot that morning to give my last official interview as one of the two producers of Disney's *A Wrinkle in Time* based on the beloved children's classic by Madeleine L'Engle. In 1963, her book received the Newbery Award for children's literature and has remained on many all-time best lists, including the New York Public Library's list of 100 Great Children's Book in 100 Years.

The film had been directed by Ava DuVernay (*Selma*) and written by Jennifer Lee (*Frozen*), starring Oprah Winfrey, Reese Witherspoon, Mindy Kaling, Chris Pine, Gugu Mbatha-Raw, and Storm Reid as the central character, Meg Murry. Ava made cinematic history when she became the first woman of color to direct a film with a budget over $100 million.

Before I left the lot that day, I asked if it was possible to see Mr. Disney's office. I knew it had been recreated to look like it did the day he died on December 15, 1966. As I stepped through the doorway, it felt like I had taken a wrinkle in time.

Mr. Disney's office was a treasure trove of beautifully maintained mid-century furniture with a photo on the wall depicting what would one day become Epcot Center in Florida. I felt a kid-like rush of excitement seeing his baby grand piano where I imagined he first heard the music for *Mary Poppins*. Directly behind it was a bookshelf that often appeared in the introductions he did for his TV series *The Wonderful World of Color*. I half expected an animated Donald Duck to pop out from one of the books.

As soon as my eyes landed on his desk, I searched for where incoming mail would have been placed. I had written a letter to him in the fall of 1963 immediately after I read *A Wrinkle in Time* on a dark and windy night. I thought Walt Disney should make a movie based on this amazing book, but I was too shy to send it. I cried when he died a few years later and felt such regret that I hadn't sent my letter; a movie now seemed impossible with his passing. I made a promise to myself on that day in 1966 to make the film when I grew up.

It was March 1979, thirteen years after I had made that promise to myself, and I was late for my first meeting with Madeleine L'Engle. As I pushed through the glass door to the lobby of the North Tower of the World Trade Center in New York City, I saw her standing near the elevator. She was taller than I expected and wore flowing layers of colorful clothing. I was grateful that she was waiting patiently—which was not something she did easily for anyone, I later learned.

I was meeting with Madeleine to discuss the possibility of optioning the film rights to her treasured book. As we headed up to the restaurant Windows on the World, I practically had an out-of-body experience being in the same elevator with her. It was the first time I had ever met with anyone about a possible film option for anything, and I wanted so desperately to succeed in getting her to trust me as the champion for the film. In truth, not just me but Norman Lear as well, one of the most successful producers in Hollywood at the time—and my boss. Years later, I learned that Madeleine agreed to the meeting because she had never been to the restaurant. I had arranged our first meeting atop the tallest building in the world because it seemed like the perfect place to discuss a tale about the mysteries of the universe.

The restaurant had a marvelous view of the Manhattan skyline, but it was so high up! As the maître d' led us to a table next to a window I asked if we could sit a few feet away since I have a fear of heights, which made Madeleine laugh. As we settled in, she leaned across the table and said with such certainty, "You know, there really is such a thing as a tesseract." I didn't know what to say. She sounded so much like Mrs Whatsit, one of the three otherworldly spirits that guide the central characters in *A Wrinkle in Time* on their cosmic journey. I never considered that a tesseract—a way to travel in the fifth dimension—existed. It took me four decades to learn that it does, although not in the way I originally thought she meant.

As I stood in Mr. Disney's office recalling that long-ago conversation with Madeleine, the resident archivist motioned me towards a glass case containing a few special items, including Mr. Disney's tweed fedora hat. The archivist also mentioned that the Walt Disney Library holds all the scripts and other materials from its various productions. I haltingly asked, "You mean, you will have a script of *A Wrinkle in Time* with my name on it in the Walt Disney Library?"

"Yes," he said. That's when it hit me; I had done it. I made my childhood dream come true—it had only taken fifty years or thereabouts.

As I left Mr. Disney's office that hot day in May, I had a deep sense of satisfaction, but once inside my car I burst into tears, feeling the weight of all that I had accomplished and endured. Over the years, my journey had moments of pure joy, myriad unexpected challenges, and considerable heartache. My goal had been to become a film producer, but along the way it morphed into something much more than that. It wasn't just about producing a movie, but also about the opportunities to learn from the people I met who inspired me to make the impossible possible.

In the film adaptation, Meg doubts her abilities to find her missing father. Mrs Which, the oldest of the celestial beings, turns to her and says, "Be a Warrior! Can you?"

This is my story of how I became a warrior.

1

Dear Mr. Disney

First, *think*. Second, *dream*.
Third, *believe*. And, finally, *dare*.

WALT DISNEY

Y ou have to have pants made of steel to be in this business and be able to take a nuclear bullet if you want to get anything done in this town," said Jerry Perenchio. It was 1976, and like any bright young twenty-four-year-old woman, I nodded in agreement as if I knew what he was talking about. Mr. Perenchio (no one ever called him anything but "Mr. Perenchio") embodied the glamour and panache of an old-fashioned Hollywood agent turned producer and entertainment executive. He had been a prominent agent in the 1960s and was the force behind launching Elton John's career in the United States in 1970. He had produced the famous Bobby Riggs/Billie Jean King tennis match, the "Battle of the Sexes" in 1973, and was now a partner in a television company called Tandem Productions.

It takes knowing someone who knows someone's cousin to get a foot in the door in the entertainment business; through a friend of a friend I was able to get this interview. Dressed in my cream-colored pantsuit with a crisp white blouse, I had high hopes that Mr. Perenchio would be able to open the door for my career in show business. Our meeting took place in his corner office in Century City—a newly built business district on the Westside of Los Angeles. As a student at Beverly Hills High, I had watched the construction of Century City from the athletic field and wondered who wanted to have an office in a building made of glass and steel. Now here I was just a few years later looking out of Mr. Perenchio's floor-to-ceiling glass window with that athletic field in the distance.

I spent my first year of college at Northwestern University just outside of Chicago, then transferred to UCLA and graduated in 1976 with a degree in theater. I was eager to do something with my life. "Let me tell you what I will do," Mr. Perenchio said. "I am going to call over and have you meet the head of personnel at Metromedia Studios. Norman Lear is doing great things over there."

Norman Lear. I had heard that name a few years earlier at the home of longtime family friends, Gene and Roz Wyman. The Wyman's home in Bel Air looked like a glamorous movie set behind black gates with a long circular driveway and an impressive fountain in front of the house. Roz had one of those smiles that lit up her face when we met her at the door and she said, "Welcome!" She had been the youngest city council member in Los Angeles history, and was credited as the person most responsible for bringing the Brooklyn Dodgers to the city. I admired Roz; she was one of the few mothers I knew who also had a career. Gene Wyman was a prominent lawyer and very active in Democratic politics, which was how our families met.

My dad, Lloyd Hand, had worked as assistant to then Senate Majority Leader Lyndon Johnson prior to our move to Los Angeles in 1961. When Johnson became vice president, Dad would often travel with him when he was on the West Coast. In some circles Dad was known as "Johnson's man in California," and he quickly became a leader in the state Democratic Party alongside Gene Wyman.

Every Sunday night, my family—Dad; my mother, Ann Hand; and my four younger brothers and sisters, Chip, Susie, Bridget, Tom, and I—would go to the Wyman's house along with other guests to watch a newly released motion picture. Everyone found a place on one of the couches or comfortable floor pillows and waited as Mr. Wyman magically turned their living room into a screening room. He always sat at one end of the sofa and leaned over to speak through an intercom to the projectionist behind the living room wall. When he'd say, "We're ready to roll!" the screen would descend from the ceiling and the opening music began. I loved it.

One weekend, we gathered to watch the movie on a Saturday night instead of Sunday. The film started later than usual because Mr. Wyman had to finish watching his favorite TV show, *All in the Family*. "It's the best thing on television," he said. "It's just outrageous. Brilliant. Genius. Never seen anything like it."

We all crammed into their small den to watch the end of the episode and I thought it funny that the main character, Archie Bunker, had the same last name as our next-door neighbors on Groverton Place, the street where I grew up in Los Angeles. Matter of fact, I broke my arm riding my bicycle down Mr. Bunker's driveway. Vice President Johnson had come for a visit, and while he met with my parents and their friends, I was showing off for the Secret Service agents parked outside, riding my bike down a hill with "no hands." It didn't go as planned. I thought of that moment as I watched the end credits roll and saw the names Norman Lear and Bud Yorkin for the first time.

Living in that house on Groverton Place was one of the happiest times in my life. I was eight years old when we moved to California after spending my very early years moving back and forth between Austin, Texas, and Washington, DC. Everything seemed greener in LA and it was more exciting living in the land of movie stars and sunshine. We lived in a big white house with black shutters framing the front windows that stood at the end of a cul-de-sac that was always filled with kids—my siblings along with neighborhood children and a constant influx of friends from school. Climbing trees was a great passion of mine and we had the best climbing tree in our front yard. The street was near Marymount High School, and my mother always said that she felt a special kind of inner peace every time she drove by the statue of the Sacred Heart that guarded the entrance to the school.

Our house was often filled with music. My mother had studied to be an opera singer, and my goal was to learn to play the piano well enough to accompany her when she sang. I had a long road ahead of me, because I hated piano lessons and would hide in a closet as soon as my piano teacher arrived. My brother Chip, only a year and a half younger than I, had mom's talent for singing. He taught himself guitar and I loved to listen to both of them. My sisters and I would dance around the living room when mom played one of her favorite tunes on the stereo, and I'm sure my love of musicals, Frank Sinatra, and Perry Como came from listening to her records.

I must have led a very sheltered life in Texas, because I had never seen a bagel until my new neighbor and new best friend, Lauren, offered me one shortly after we moved there. Every day after school and on weekends, Lauren and I would go on adventures in the neighborhood. We discovered that Jane Withers, a depression-era child actress who made several movies with Shirley Temple, lived down the street, but we never saw her and not because we didn't try. We would scale the fence hidden under tall hedges surrounding her house. The sweet smell of the honeysuckle that covered the hedges was our only compensation for the scratches that would inevitably result.

In 1962 during the Cuban Missile Crisis, our next-door neighbor built a bomb shelter, and I could never understand how something built above ground was going to protect him from a nuclear attack. Dad revealed just a few years ago that during that time LBJ had asked my parents to meet him at the Los Angeles airport. As they sat in their car on the tarmac near his plane while it was being refueled, Johnson said, "You know, Annie, you all need to go stock up on water and all essential foods." He knew that we were that close to being in a war; my parents followed his advice and stocked up on supplies. Food was flying off the shelves, because people thought there really was going to be a nuclear war. It was a scary time. We had duck-and-cover drills at school and were told not to go near the windows in case we came under attack. Those drills seem so naïve today—that somehow hiding under a desk was going to protect us from a nuclear bomb.

It was in that house on Groverton Place in the fall of 1963 that I first read *A Wrinkle in Time.* The Santa Ana winds, unusually fierce dry winds that bluster in autumn and spring in Southern California, blew through the open windows. American novelist Raymond Chandler described the Santa Anas as ". . . Those hot dry [winds] that come down through the mountain passes and curl your hair and make your nerves jump and your skin itch. On nights like that every booze party ends in a fight. Meek little wives feel the edge of the carving knife and study their husbands' necks. Anything can happen." That night something definitely did.

The hand-cranked windows that lined the walls of the room in our home that we called the office were wide open and I could feel the hot dry air of the Santa Ana winds swirling around me. Curled up in an overstuffed chair, I opened my book and read, "It was a dark and stormy night. In her attic bedroom Margaret Murry, wrapped in an old patchwork quilt, sat on the foot of her bed and watched the trees tossing in the frenzied lashing of the wind. Wrapped in her quilt, Meg shook." That night, my world shook and I was never the same again.

Earlier that day, my fifth-grade teacher told me I had to improve my reading. At recess, my friend Lauren beat all the boys in handball; I paled in comparison. On top of everything else, I had been sent to the library that afternoon for talking in class. I felt like I did everything wrong. As I sat quietly at one of the round tables, a kindly librarian, her auburn hair tied up in a knot, came over to me. She asked what kind of books I liked to read. "I don't like to read," I said. I much preferred handball. Reading was so boring, I thought.

"Ah, but you might like *A Wrinkle in Time*. It won this year's Newbery Award for children's literature and it's about a girl just like you." I asked, "What's the Newbery Award?" And she replied, "It's the best book written this year for someone your age." The blue cover with green rings around three children seemed mysterious. When I opened a random page, I saw the word *October*. My birthday is in October, so on the basis of that, I said I would give it a try.

The Murry family lived in a big white house just outside a small New England town. The central character, Meg Murry, is a young, insecure teenage girl whose scientist father, while working on a top-secret project called the Tesseract, has mysteriously disappeared. Officials haven't told her mother anything concerning his whereabouts, and Meg is on the verge of giving up hope he will return.

Meg's five-year-old brother, Charles Wallace, speaks and acts older than his age and has an uncanny ability to read Meg's thoughts. Twins Sandy and Dennys are typical ten-year-olds that tease their sister for taking everything so *personally*. Mrs. Murry, a microbiologist, is unafraid to question the known universe and has faith that her husband will return.

Late that night, an old woman called Mrs Whatsit knocks on the Murry kitchen door. The twins are asleep but Meg, Charles Wallace, and their mother are in the kitchen having hot cocoa. Mrs. Murry welcomes Mrs Whatsit inside to dry off. It turns out that Charles Wallace has met Mrs Whatsit along with her two friends Mrs Who and Mrs Which at the haunted house in the nearby woods. Meg is suspicious of their visitor, and their mother admonishes Charles Wallace for going into the woods without permission. As Mrs Whatsit is about to leave, she says to Mrs. Murry, "By the way, pet, there is such a thing as a tesseract." Mrs. Murry's face goes ashen. How could this old woman know about her husband's top-secret project?

Meg, Charles Wallace, and their friend Calvin are swept up into a cosmic journey guided by the celestial creatures Mrs Whatsit, Mrs Who, and Mrs Which. They travel to find Dr. Murry who has been captured on Camazotz, a planet that has succumbed to the darkness. The people on Camazotz have given up their ability to think for themselves and have turned to the ominous Man with the Red Eyes for salvation.

The children's journey is one of self-discovery. Meg learns that her "faults" are the very strengths she needs to bring her father home. The stakes increase when she learns that it isn't just her father's life in danger; a powerful evil force is spreading throughout the galaxies and Earth is surrounded by Darkness. There is a glimmer of hope; fighters on Earth are holding the darkness at bay. In Meg's climactic fight to save Charles Wallace, she learns that unconditional love can overcome the darkness.

As the winds blew that night, I fell in love. When I read that Meg Murry wanted to get rid of her faults, I knew exactly how she felt. The librarian was right; A Wrinkle in Time was about a girl just like me. Meg's mother said that her father was away on a top-secret mission; my father would often start conversations with "This needs to stay in the family," which I heard as "top-secret." The walk Meg and her brother Charles Wallace took through the woods behind their house felt familiar—my siblings and I would also go exploring in the woods behind our house. Like Meg's love interest, the red-haired Calvin, I had a crush on a tall, red-haired boy in my class.

Most especially, I understood Meg's special relationship with her youngest brother. Like Charles Wallace, my youngest brother, Tom, was different from other children his age, and I felt very protective of him. There was no name for what was wrong, but he had a hard time catching a ball or putting the right meaning to words. One time his arithmetic teacher asked him, "What is a yard?" and he replied, "Where you keep chickens." Not exactly wrong, but not exactly right, either. When he was only five years old he was the ring bearer in President Johnson's daughter Luci's wedding, which required him to walk down the long aisle at the Shrine at the Immaculate Conception Cathedral in Washington, DC. My parents breathed a sigh of relief when he walked passed them, smiled, and continued down the aisle to his designated spot, very proud of himself. Mom said he had learning disabilities, which could mean anything. I saw him as Mrs. Murry describes Charles Wallace, as simply something "new."

A Wrinkle in Time was definitely something new for me—even better than handball. It was a portal into a wondrous, mysterious universe that set my curiosity on fire. Who were Euclid, Michelangelo, and Buddha—all mentioned as fighters in the story—and what did they have in common with Jesus? Are there really other planets in the universe? What did Meg's father mean when he said that time is an illusion and energy and matter are interchangeable? What is resilience? Is it possible that stars are linked to a galactic force for good and watch over us every night? I never knew books could inspire in me the desire to find answers to so many questions.

Reading *Wrinkle* made me feel smart. My view of the universe was pocket-size compared to how I experienced a wrinkle in time—traveling in the fifth dimension meant there must be a fourth and maybe a sixth. I discovered that it is how we use our talents that counts, and that a girl—even a girl who was trying to get rid of her faults—could be a hero. Most significantly, the book gave me hope when President Kennedy was assassinated.

The year 1963 was fraught with explosive events that became topics of ongoing dinner table conversations. George Wallace became governor of Alabama and proclaimed, "Segregation now, segregation tomorrow, and segregation forever." Betty Friedan's book *The Feminine Mystique* launched the reawakening of the women's movement in the United States. Seventy thousand marchers arrived in London to demonstrate against nuclear weapons. Martin Luther King Jr. issued his "Letter from Birmingham Jail," and in August delivered his "I Have a Dream" speech from the steps of the Lincoln Memorial. The US Supreme Court ruled that state-mandated Bible reading in public schools was unconstitutional. Then on November 22, a cloud of darkness descended over the entire planet and time stopped. President Kennedy had been assassinated.

My dad had seen President Kennedy the day before on the tarmac at the Houston airport. He had been at the LBJ ranch and was at the airport to fly home when a friend of his who was advancing the Kennedy/Johnson trip to Texas suggested he come over and say hello to them. While he didn't know Mrs. Kennedy, he had campaigned with President Kennedy when he was in Texas and found him to be very charming. Dad was in his office in LA when someone called to say that the president had been shot. The following day he flew to DC with Gene Wyman. They immediately went to the Old Executive Building and were with Johnson when he was on the phone putting together the Warren Commission. A few hours later, Dad attended Kennedy's funeral at St. Matthews. As he tells it, it was beyond heartbreaking from both a personal and public perspective. No one could understand why anyone would want to kill this extraordinary man.

I spent hours with my mom and siblings gathered around the TV. We watched as Jack Ruby shot Lee Harvey Oswald outside the Dallas police station and witnessed the moving coverage of the funeral. Along with millions of people around the world, we listened to the endless drums, watched the horseless rider, cried as John-John saluted his father's casket and as Mrs. Kennedy lit the eternal flame—images that would last a lifetime. I was frightened to hear adults say that inno-cence and hope had died; *Wrinkle* helped me understand that while darkness exists, it can be overcome. The book gave me the courage I needed in those melancholy days.

I finished the book in late November and immediately started my letter to Walt Disney. The letter started with some-thing like, "Dear Mr. Disney, Please make a movie of *A Wrinkle in Time* and star me as Meg." I can still feel the pencil in my hand as I tried to write the words and keep them in a straight line, but I was too shy to send it. I put the pencil down, crum-pled the piece of paper into a ball, and tossed it into the trash. I thought, Why send it when he probably won't read it?

Reading *A Wrinkle in Time* wasn't the only life-changing event that took place on Groverton Place. My brother Chip started showing signs of a medical condition. My parents never knew precisely what it was—he had asthma-like symp-toms—but they did everything they knew to do to help him. He coughed incessantly and would become so sweaty from the effort that my parents often had to rush him to UCLA Hospital. The doctors would put him in an oxygen tent that stopped the coughing for a few days, but then it would resume. Chip was my best buddy in childhood and I hated to see him suffer. While he could be annoying at times like any younger brother could be, he was smart, extremely funny, and looked up to me as his big sister.

Chip and I shared a love of old movies and would wake up at the crack of dawn when everyone else was asleep and race down to our one TV in the den. We played a game of "I got dibs on the TV"—whoever got to the television first could decide what we would watch. Sometimes it was a draw, but more often than not Chip won. I can still hear him shout with glee, "I won! I won!" The local stations ran old movies early in the morning. To this day, I have such sweet memories of sitting on the couch next to Chip watching films from the 1930s and '40s.

I was mesmerized by the actresses of that era and lived vicariously through the heroines they played. Barbara Stanwyck, Katharine Hepburn, Greer Garson, Olivia de Havilland, Ingrid Bergman, Bette Davis, and Rosalind Russell taught me how to be a strong independent-minded woman. There were also the great actresses in old musicals like Judy Garland, Ginger Rogers, Betty Grable, June Allyson, Alice Faye, and so many others. They made me laugh and want to learn how to sing and dance; they provided a feeling of pure joy. These marvelous women influenced my life; they helped me dream about whom I wanted to be when I grew up.

My dreams never included another move back to Washington, DC, but that is what happened in January 1965. After Johnson won the presidential election in November, he called Dad during the Christmas holiday and asked him to be his White House chief of protocol, which carried with it the rank of ambassador. Johnson told him, "I want you to come back and help Bill [Moyers] and Jack [Valenti] and me run this White House. It's going to take a new set of luggage on your part. It's like always before. You'll have to do all kinds of things. You'll have to open doors for these diplomats." I remember that call vividly, because my grandparents on my father's side were thrilled that the president of the United States was on the phone with their son. It was quite a moment

At Dad's swearing-in to become chief of protocol, January 1965.
I'm on his right with Mom behind him, Bridget, Chip
and Susie to his left, and Tom front and center.

for two people who had never graduated from high school to
have their son do so well.

It was an exciting opportunity for both my parents, but
not so much for my siblings and me. I was in seventh grade
and had just started junior high school. It was a time fraught
with uncertainty, lack of self-confidence, and insecurity
about who I was in the grand scheme of things. In home-
room right before class started, a boy sitting behind me said,

"With a father as smart as yours and a mother that is so beautiful, what happened to you?" It was a question that I often asked myself in those days. I loved my parents and wanted to please them, but moving to DC meant leaving behind my friends and making new ones in what seemed to me a foreign land in the middle of the seventh grade. When I complained, my mom's response was "you have to learn to be flexible." I didn't want to be flexible.

I would come to learn in this new foreign land that it would also be hard to compete with the president of the United States for my parents' attention. There were trade-offs, although a kid doesn't always see it like that. President Johnson depended on Dad to handle any matters pertaining to diplomacy and the State Department, which meant that both my parents were sent abroad on Air Force One around the world representing the president. As a result, our parents had great stories to share with us that I loved to hear and they loved to tell. Dad's first assignment was to attend Winston Churchill's funeral as part of the official US delegation with Chief Justice Earl Warren and our ambassador to Great Britain, David Bruce. President Johnson was recovering from pneumonia and couldn't attend, and neither could Secretary of State Dean Rusk.

Dad had such a great memory for detail and shared how magnificent everything was—including that he stood just a few feet away from the historic figures who were there to pay their respects, including Charles de Gaulle and former Prime Minister Clement Attlee. Churchill had scripted his own funeral, so the ceremony was very precise. When the program said that the casket of the prime minister would be placed on the caisson at the strike of ten o'clock at Westminster—the casket was placed on the caisson the moment the clock struck ten o'clock. The thing that really moved my father was how respectful and somber the British citizens were who lined the streets four or five people deep.

President Johnson called Dad in London after the funeral was concluded, and said, "Lloyd, I'm sending a plane to bring President Eisenhower back. He was a great friend of Churchill's and he is with two of his friends. Just look after them. I would appreciate it." My father got out to the airport early and saw a gorgeous woman in matching sable hat and coat walking towards him. "Hello, my name is Pamela Hayward and I'm to meet President Eisenhower," she said. Pamela Hayward would go on to marry Averell Harriman, our top diplomat working with the Soviet Union during the Cold War, and she would eventually become our ambassador to France. Once on board, President Eisenhower asked Dad if he would like to join him, Pamela, and another woman in a game of bridge on the flight home. Much to Dad's disappointment he had to decline—he had never learned the game. A Secret Service agent sat in instead.

There were lots of stories like that: their last-minute trip to the Paris Air Show with Vice President Humphrey and the first US astronauts to walk in space, Ed White and Jim McDivitt; arranging President Johnson's visit with Pope Paul VI in New York; picking up Princess Margaret and Lord Snowdon to take them to the White House dinner in their honor; and traveling with Vice President Humphrey on his nine-nation tour meeting with our allies during the Vietnam

War. I loved learning that Dad was tasked with escorting the pope to the Waldorf Astoria hotel to meet with President Johnson. I asked, "You mean you rode in the car sitting next to the pope?!" He nodded. "What did you talk about?" He couldn't remember, because he was too worried about the thousands of people lining the streets who at any moment could crush them.

The nine-nation tour to Japan, Korea, Pakistan, India, Laos, Philippines, Australia, Thailand, and New Zealand was eye opening for him. Every head of state told Vice President Humphrey that they supported the US role, but wouldn't say so publicly. Hearing this must have been the first time I learned that public statements aren't necessarily the truth. And I couldn't get over the fact that Dad sat across from Indira Gandhi, the first female prime minister of India. I'm sure my love of story and history started when hearing Mom and Dad describe the people they met and the places they visited. Their stories made everything so real, not simply names in books or on the news, but because they had been in the room with these people. My parents' respect for the extraordinary individuals they met made a huge impression on me. Their stories gave me a perspective about fame and achievement that would last a lifetime. Famous people were just like us—normal people who found themselves in extraordinary situations and rose to the challenge.

It was during this time that I had my first experience with the press. *Life Magazine* did a seven-page story on my parents as the new attractive young family in DC representing LBJ with the diplomatic community. Mom was quite beautiful and LBJ once joked in front of about fifteen society reporters that

Mom was the real reason he brought Dad to Washington. She was just thirty-two years old and rose to the challenge, handling their social obligations while raising five young children. The headline of the article ended up reading: "The Chief of Protocol AND HIS WIFE."

Another news outlet did a feature story on, of all things, my bedroom decor. "Cathy Hand reigns over her own small blue and white domain in her family's suburban Virginia home with a tidy hand. A sports-loving but feminine tomboy with an effervescent friendliness." The article stands out in my mind because of the request made by the photographer that day. He asked, "Do you have a favorite book you would like

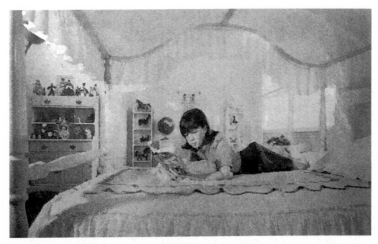

"A sports-loving but feminine tomboy with
an effervescent friendliness," October 1965
PHOTO COURTESY OF GOODYEAR CO.

to hold while I take a picture of you reading on your bed?" I frantically searched my bookshelf that had once belonged to my mom when she was a young girl, looking for my copy of *A Wrinkle in Time.* Then it dawned on me that I had checked it out of the library and didn't own a copy. I grabbed a Nancy Drew book instead, but was always a little disappointed that the photo didn't show me reading *Wrinkle.*

My early teenage years weren't normal, but they were *my* normal. One minute I'd be obsessing over the length of my bangs, and the next I'd be asked to put on a nice dress because the wife of the president of some country was stopping by to see an American family. I was learning the art of diplomacy at the age of twelve, but mostly I was a kid trying to fit in with my new classmates and spending hours with my friend Mary trying to decipher the meaning of the lyrics to the song, "Louie, Louie." Turning thirteen felt like the end of my world as I knew it; I was upset about leaving my childhood behind and becoming a teenager. At one point, I sat next to my mom on the living room couch and wept, "I'll never be able to climb a tree again." She assured me that it wasn't all that bad. I think the tears also had something to do with the fact that both my parents would be in Africa on my actual birthday.

As a way to soften what I saw as a terrible oversight on their part, they surprised me a few weeks before their trip with a special dinner at the F Street Club. The restaurant glowed with warm candlelight. As we were escorted to our table, I saw there were other adults already seated. After a few minutes, Vice President Humphrey walked in and I was surprised to find that he was my dinner companion. He pulled up his chair next to mine and handed me a birthday present—a beautiful gold charm bracelet. I was thrilled that he wanted to know what I thought about everything. Afterwards, our small dinner party went to Constitution Hall to hear the great pianist Van Cliburn play. We sat in the presidential box and Vice President Humphrey pulled my chair up between him and Mrs. Humphrey. During intermission, I followed my parents and the Humphreys into a beautiful reception area and met Van Cliburn. As I shook his hand and found my entire hand fit into his palm, I realized that it was a good thing I had decided against becoming a concert pianist.

It was while living in Washington, DC, that I realized just how impactful *Wrinkle* had been on me. I identified with Meg's yearning to find her father who would make everything better, but it was the scene when the children learn about "the fighters" that resonated with me in an enduring way. The idea of fighting back darkness and spreading light made sense to me when listening to my parents' stories about Martin Luther King Jr. and his fight for civil rights, Lyndon Johnson's war on poverty, and so many other fighters whose names I heard around the dinner table, in the news, and from guests in our home. Fighters were not just in the past but also in the present, and I saw anyone who fought injustice or tried to make the world a better place as just that: a fighter.

By the middle of eighth grade, I had finally started to make a few good friends—and just as I settled into our life in DC, I was told we were moving back to California. At the urging of several friends in Los Angeles, Dad had decided to run for lieutenant governor in the 1966 governor's race—the year

Ronald Reagan won. Even though it meant leaving friends behind again, we were all happy to move back home, though it wouldn't be to our house on Groverton Place. We took up temporary residency at a house on the beach in Santa Monica that once belonged to Cary Grant. When Chip and I heard that, we must have walked every inch of that house saying to ourselves, "Cary Grant walked here." We also were enlisted as volunteers for my dad's campaign and had to distribute flyers on all the cars parked at the beach near our home. Thankfully, Dad lost the primary, Ronald Reagan became governor, and we returned to a regular life.

We left Santa Monica by the time school began in the fall of 1966 and moved to a lovely home in the flats of Beverly Hills just above Santa Monica Boulevard. It was a stone covered house with a white picket fence that Mom made sure was eventually covered in roses. Our home was once again filled with music, constant entertaining, and kids coming and going. My parents had a diverse group of friends that came from the world of entertainment and politics. People told Dad that he should run for mayor of Los Angeles, but he had no interest in running for another office. Mom founded a nonprofit organization called Learn and Return to support children who had emotional and mental health issues like Tom. Through that effort, she acquired a reputation of helping those in the community and made good friends who were very prominent. She was asked to join SHARE, an organization comprised mainly of entertainers and wives of entertainers. It was an impressive and fun group of women and introduced mom to the world of show business.

Sadly, Chip's persistent cough made it difficult for him to live with us, so he attended a boarding school in Arizona for a while. Doctors could never understand what caused the cough, but it didn't occur in drier climates. Tommy was in a special school for children with learning disabilities. My younger sisters started a new elementary school, and I began my freshman year at Beverly Hills High, which I hated at first. Beverly was my fourteenth school by the time I was fourteen, and even though I had learned to become more flexible, I hated being the new kid yet again. My mother reminded me that I wasn't the only one feeling awkward and I should smile when I felt unsure of myself, which I tried to do, if grudgingly.

In December of 1966, my freshman year at Beverly, Walt Disney died. I remember hearing the news while standing outside the house and didn't want anyone to see me cry. I went inside and took the stairs two steps at a time to get to my bedroom before I fell apart. It's beyond me why I felt such loss for someone I had never met. It really felt like he was our Uncle Walt, welcomed into our home every Sunday night when we watched his television show *The Wonderful World of Color*. I thought that Mr. Disney really understood a kid's love for adventure. Trips to Disneyland were an annual summer tradition when my parents' friends would come for a visit. I especially loved Tom Sawyer Island. As I sat there on the bed sobbing, I felt such regret that I didn't send that letter to him about *A Wrinkle in Time*. I contemplated sending a letter to someone else, but knew of no one else who made films for children. The only thing for me to do, I reasoned, was to grow up and get the film made myself. Walt Disney once said, "First, *think*. Second, *dream*. Third, *believe*. And, finally, *dare*." And that is what I took to heart at fourteen years of age.

I held back from mentioning this dream to my friends in high school, because our collective focus was on more important things like the draft and the ongoing Vietnam War. The possibility of being drafted was very real, and once my friends found out that Dad had worked with Johnson, they had numerous heated conversations with him over the war. By the time 1968 rolled around, it felt like we were living in the midst of a revolution. We all lived with an odd balance of typical high school activities like auditioning for the school play and then gathering to march against the war at UCLA with fellow protestors. Dad asked me if I wanted to study the law when I went to college, but I told him I wanted to be in the entertainment business. I believed it was important to change attitudes before changing laws, and I was becoming more aware of how movies like *Guess Who's Coming to Dinner* helped to change attitudes.

Social discontent and anger about the war exploded at the 1968 Democratic Convention. Almost all of my high school friends were in favor of candidates Bobby Kennedy or Eugene McCarthy, and I probably would have been, too, except that dad was close to Humphrey. Just before my parents were to leave for the convention in Chicago that summer, Mom asked if I would like to accompany them. She said, "It will be a memorable experience for you," not having a clue about what lay ahead.

Bob Squier, Humphrey's communications advisor, asked me to be the gofer for his communications team so I would have something to do while my parents were off in meetings.

As I ran errands for him, I quickly learned how to navigate my way through the hordes of people walking the hallways of the Conrad Hilton Hotel. I soon discovered that I had the superpower of invisibility because no one ever stopped a young teenage girl for her ID. This made it possible for me to go anywhere in the hotel as well as the International Amphitheater where the convention took place.

As the week progressed, it was shocking to see the violence and unrest. Mayor Daley's decision to bring in the National Guard resulted in horrible treatment of the protestors. My parents were terrified as they sat in their car when it was overtaken by an angry mob outside the convention center. By that point, the demonstrators were more upset with the brutality of Mayor Daley's show of force than anything else. My sweet adventure of navigating the hallways in the hotel became an exercise in finding alternative routes to escape the foul odor of stink bombs.

I saw the vice president one more time at our home in Los Angeles that November. It was the night before the presidential election and Dad had helped organize a major star-studded telethon for the Humphrey campaign followed by a big thank you party for 400 people at our home. A big tent covered our backyard and the house was filled with red, white, and blue balloons that my brother Tom thought were for him because he turned eight years old that day. There were all sorts of celebrities, volunteers, and members of the press. I particularly recall seeing Ryan O'Neal. My sisters and I were fans of the hugely popular TV series *Peyton Place* and over the moon excited to meet Rodney Harrington, the character O'Neal played, in person. Unfortunately, it wasn't an early victory

party. Humphrey lost the election the next day and Richard
Nixon became our 37th president.

My mother's advice had been right about smiling when I felt
awkward. For the first time in my life I was able to stay in a
school for four uninterrupted years and made loads of friends.
My senior year was filled with one activity after another. I was
the student body secretary, lead in the school play, and senior
princess for the invitational basketball tournament. Out of
the blue, I was asked to escort *Life Magazine* photographers
around campus for a story they were doing on the current
high school dress styles. They asked me to get into the very last
photo they took that day, and I was surprised to find it made
it into the article (see page 30). I was shocked to be voted Most
Likely to Succeed and humbled that my friends saw me in
that way. It's funny how my understanding of success would
change a dozen times over the following decades.

I was ecstatic when I got accepted to Northwestern University
located just outside of Chicago. I had lived in the South and on
both East and West coasts, and wanted to know what it was like
to live in the Midwest. Northwestern was known for its theater
program, which was my major along with a minor in politics
and religion. I had grown fascinated with how the three areas
seemed intertwined and was curious to know more. A mysterious thing happened to me, though, in the winter of '71 that
precipitated a transfer to UCLA the following fall.

On February 10, 1971, I woke up in my dorm room to the
radio announcement that there had been a devastating 6.6

Beverly Hills High School, October 1969.
(I'm the one with white knee socks.)

earthquake in Los Angeles. My parents were in the Philippines at the time, but my siblings were at our home in LA. I called to see if everyone was okay and then ran to class. That afternoon as I was walking back to the dorm with a few friends, I slipped on the ice, landing on my back. I went to see the nurse at the health center and she sent me to Evanston Hospital. As I walked towards the entrance to the hospital, I collapsed and was paralyzed from my neck down.

The doctors took X-rays, moved my legs up and down, but no one could figure out what was wrong. My parents were contacted and Dad flew directly to Chicago, arriving that night at the hospital. This was when everything became very strange. The doctor came in and told us that I had hysterical paralysis. I had no idea what that meant, only that it implied that the paralysis was all in my head; I felt embarrassed and ashamed for doing something so ridiculous. I immediately set about sending commands to my legs, feet, and arms to move, but they wouldn't. Then fear set in. Why wouldn't my legs move when I commanded my body to "move," if it was in my head? Dad stayed by my side, but Mom had taken ill in the Philippines and couldn't leave the hospital there. A few days went by and I started to have some movement in my arms and within a week recovered the use of my legs. The best anyone could piece together was that I had felt so conflicted about not being in LA with my brothers and sisters during the earthquake that I literally became paralyzed.

The day we left the hospital, I was wheeled into a small amphitheater and questioned by several doctors trying to learn more about hysterical paralysis. My doctor said something to me before we left for which I have been forever grateful. He said, "Dumb people don't do what you did. Never let anyone tell you that you aren't smart." I felt like I was stupid for doing something that I thought was so dumb, but his comment really mattered to me, especially when I returned home. The great takeaway was what I learned about the unimaginable power of the brain. Nothing like it ever happened again. I stayed at Northwestern to finish my year there, but I was ready to return to warmer weather and continued my studies at UCLA.

Between my junior and senior year, I took a break from school and moved to Washington, DC, to explore the possibility of a career in politics rather than entertainment. I was twenty years old with absolutely no experience and didn't even know what members of Congress did on a daily basis but was determined to find out. Humphrey had returned to the Senate in 1970, and two years later, I was on his calendar to meet about possible job opportunities on Capitol Hill. As I waited outside his office, the receptionist was exceptionally kind, and after a short while, the senator appeared and greeted me in his ever-ebullient way, "Hello, Cathy! Welcome!" I wondered how he could still be so enthusiastic after he had to withstand the slings and arrows of the brutal 1968 presidential campaign. His attitude and approach to life made a lasting impression on me that day.

After I told him about my interest in working on Capitol Hill, he said, "You know, Cathy, my receptionist is one of the most important people in my office. A great receptionist is hard to find. If my receptionist makes my constituents feel welcome when they come to my office, it makes any meeting with them so much easier." It was true that his receptionist had made me feel less anxious about meeting with him. And he had a genuine sense of gratitude for everyone who worked with him—he made it seem like all jobs in an office had value, whether you were the receptionist or the chief of staff. Eventually I found a job working for Senator Mike Gravel from Alaska and stayed in DC for thirteen months.

Four years later, thanks to Mr. Perenchio, I sat across from the head of personnel at Tandem Productions and was offered the position of receptionist in Norman Lear's office at Metromedia Studios. I was thrilled to take the job, knowing how Humphrey had viewed the position of receptionist. I was a little disappointed that my first job in entertainment would be in television and not in movies, but at least it was with the company that produced *All in the Family*, the series Mr. Wyman thought was brilliant.

In my job, I answered the phone as if the person on the other end was the most important person in the world. One morning, the phone rang and I said, "Good morning, Norman Lear's office." The person on the other end of the line asked, "Who is this?" I said, "Cathy Hand—I'm the receptionist." To which the caller replied, "This is Norman Lear and I've never heard anyone say good morning like that." He was making a joke, but my twenty-four-year-old self heard that he was pleased with how I answered the phone. That was my first conversation with Norman Lear, and the beginning of my journey to bring *A Wrinkle in Time* to the screen.

2
Another Letter

Laughter adds years to your life.

NORMAN LEAR

I t only took a few days on the job to discover that Tandem was one of the hottest—if not *the* hottest— production company in Los Angeles at the time. *All in the Family* was a megahit of the first order. It would go on to win twenty-two Emmys on fifty-five nominations. Sixty million people tuned in every week to laugh at the outrageous quarrels between the loveable bigot Archie Bunker and his liberal son-in-law, Mike "Meathead" Stivic. His long-suffering wife, Edith, and daughter, Gloria, tried to keep the peace. The family quarrels were over many issues that people across the country were struggling to grapple with in their own families—the Vietnam War, racism, abortion, and homosexuality—but no one had ever tackled these topics in a situation comedy. The series held a mirror up to the chaos and divisiveness of the era and helped us see not only the humor in our differences, but that we can vehemently disagree and still get along.

By the time I started working at Metromedia Studios, Norman was supervising five prime time series in addition to *All in the Family*: *The Jeffersons, Maude, One Day at a Time, Good Times,* and the late-night cult hit, *Mary Hartman, Mary Hartman,* with several more series to follow. Bud Yorkin, his partner and co-creator of *All in the Family,* was located at the Burbank Studios producing the huge hit *Sanford and Son* and developing film projects. Between them, Norman and Bud had seven series—often in the weekly top ten. I had no idea how unusual it was for one production company to be responsible for that many television series at the same time.

Many of the best writers, directors, and actors in town wanted to be a part of the great things Norman was doing. Writers like Bob Weiskopf and Bob Schiller, who were seasoned veterans from such comedy classics as *Make Room for Daddy* with Danny Thomas, and *I Love Lucy*, went on to make history with their work on *All in the Family*. They were instrumental in hiring a young writer named Charlie Hauck who wrote some of the funniest lines on TV for *Maude*. I have always thought that Norman's secret sauce for so much success was that he often paired veterans like Schiller and Weiskopf with new talent like Charlie—they all learned from each other.

The best thing about so much success was the activity it generated in both the offices and the rehearsal halls leading up to the designated tape day. There were two tapings for every episode—one at five-thirty and another at eight in the evening in front of live audiences—and the show that aired was a combination of the two. Up-and-coming comedians competed to do the warm-up in front of the audiences (to get them laughing before the show began), and I remember a certain buzz around one of the guys named Michael Keaton. Charlie Hauck had encouraged Keaton to move to Los Angeles and helped him get the chance to perform.

My desk was next to the main door, which gave me the perfect spot to get to know all who entered the executive suite. The writers and producers of a series met with Norman every week around his conference table to talk through the ideas for the episode. There were two other secretaries across from me in the main lobby area, and if we weren't too busy, we were laughing with the writers waiting for their meeting to begin. There is nothing better than to work around comedy writers because they are wicked funny, and we laughed a lot. Norman would hear the laughter and have to check out what was going on, and would join in with some funny remark or fake a fall to get more laughter. He often said, "Laughter adds years to your life," and we all added years to our lives back then.

Sitting at my desk or walking the hallways, I would often overhear the struggles the writers and producers dealt with on a weekly basis—script problems, an actor complaining about his or her character, a set that was causing trouble, and budget constraints. I also came to see that Norman never shied away from the challenge of finding humor in the tough topics explored in all of his shows. He had flown more than fifty bombing missions during World War II and became fearless in all things once he returned home. One of the toughest episodes had to have been when Edith Bunker was raped. I could hear just outside the main door how upset the writers were as they left their meeting with Norman, "How do you make rape funny? Rape is not funny." By the time the episode aired it was extremely moving and even managed to find a laugh or two.

It took hundreds of people to bring the shows to life, and everyone had a part to play. I loved my role as the receptionist, but there were times when I could have been a little less enthusiastic and more attentive to details. One moment in particular still stays with me. Orson Welles came to meet with Norman about an idea he had for a TV series. Orson Welles. *The Citizen Kane* Orson Welles. *The Jane Eyre* Orson Welles. I couldn't believe that a filmmaker of that caliber would want to develop a TV series. I was in awe of Welles and everyone in the office knew it, so they weren't surprised when I asked to greet him at the front door to our building.

As he approached the entrance I noticed right away that he had gained a lot of weight and didn't look like Charles Foster Kane or Mr. Rochester, but the voice—that voice—was there. Without thinking, I immediately led him up the one flight of stairs that I took every day. As we reached the middle landing I saw that he was having trouble breathing. He leaned on the handrail and with great difficulty said, "Don't . . . you . . . have . . . an . . . elevator?" I was mortified that I hadn't thought to take the elevator and worried I might get fired. We also hadn't anticipated the difficulty he would have sitting in the armchairs around Norman's conference table. I quickly found a chair without arms—and I didn't get fired.

While I wanted to do a good job, I also secretly hoped that I would be discovered as an actress sitting at my desk, like actress Lana Turner had been discovered while sitting at the soda fountain at Schwab's Drug Store. After all, my letter to Walt Disney about *A Wrinkle in Time* suggested having me *star* as Meg. Until I started working at Tandem Productions, I didn't know women could be anything other than a secretary or an actress in show business. My initial thought to get *Wrinkle* adapted for the screen was from the point of view of an actress. I knew that by the time I grew up I would no longer be the right age to play Meg and would have to play her mother instead.

My hero was the great actress Katharine Hepburn. She epitomized all that I hoped to be: strong, independent, talented, and successful. Of course, there also was her relationship with Spencer Tracy that I found intriguing and romantic. I would faithfully read everything I could about her and watch all her old movies dozens of times on TV. I was completely starstruck when I was in Paris and happened to see her in person. I was about to turn nineteen years old and had joined my father on one of his business trips to Paris. Paris has been referred to as the City of Light since the 1800s when it was considered the seat of enlightenment, which certainly seemed to be even more than 100 years later. I felt more enlightened just standing on a street corner.

One evening we returned to the hotel after dinner, and as I was about to head for the elevator, my dad gently tugged my sleeve and looked towards the reception desk. Standing there was Katharine Hepburn. I don't know how Dad managed it, but we lingered in the lobby long enough to get in the same elevator with her. However, I couldn't bring myself to raise my head—I didn't want to be caught staring. The next day, I spent the morning sitting in the lobby of the Hotel Lancaster waiting for her to exit the hotel. I was on my first trip to Paris and wasted hours sitting in a hotel lobby! It finally dawned on me that this was not a good idea.

I knew she had gotten off on the third floor so I thought I would just magically find her room, knock on the door, and tell her how much I loved her work. As I walked the third-floor hallway, I saw a door slightly ajar and heard her voice. She was talking with someone and I came within inches of knocking, but hesitated. I was just too shy—just like when I had hesitated to send the letter to Mr. Disney.

Later that day as I walked down the Champs Elysees, two young men approached me and didn't hesitate to ask, "Aren't you Cathy Hand?" There was no internet in those days—no posting of selfies on Instagram—and no one knew I was in Paris. I was shocked that someone knew me. It turned out that six months earlier they had bought chocolate chip cookies from me at the library during my freshman year at Northwestern when I was trying to raise money for a trip to New Orleans. I was surprised and grateful that these two young men remembered me from our brief encounter, and we spent the rest of the afternoon together. Their company helped me get over the disappointment of not seeing Katharine Hepburn ever again.

My hopes for an acting career came to a screeching halt one day while working at Tandem. There was a "cattle call"—an audition for a part open to everyone—for a role that I thought was perfect for me. By lunchtime our office and the hallways were filled with young women who were exactly like my type. I wasn't so unique. I was stunned to see how much competition there was for roles and started to have second thoughts about pursing an acting career. It was at that moment that my eyes were opened to other opportunities for women in the entertainment business. A woman named Viva Knight had been hired to produce one of Norman's new shows, *All That Glitters*, about a world where women are in charge. The premise for *All that Glitters* was such a radical idea in 1977. Watching Viva in action inspired me to let go of my desire to be in front of the camera and to work towards getting behind it. I don't even think she knew my name.

There were plenty of articles written about how Norman's shows galvanized society to think differently, and they certainly pushed all of us who worked there to do the same. All my earlier prejudices about working in television went out the window the more time I spent working at Tandem and witnessed how that medium was changing attitudes as much as, or even more than, films. This was especially true when it came to how I perceived opportunities for women in the workplace. I had such limited expectations until I started watching Viva attend meetings in Norman's office. Her views influenced the direction of the show, as well as who was hired for the cast and crew. It is very common today for women to be producers, but it wasn't then. I had thought that level of leadership was only open to men, but she made me see myself not as actress, receptionist, or secretary, but as a producer.

Listening to Viva in action, I began to piece together the essential talents needed to become a producer: an eye for material—that is, an idea or property that someone wants and is willing to pay for; a knack for cultivating relationships with potential funding sources; and a curiosity and awareness of both veteran and rising writers, directors, actors, cinematographers, and production designers—all types of talent that make it possible to bring an idea to fruition. Did I have any of these talents? I thought I had an eye for good material, and I had discovered that the years I moved from school to school had honed my skills at being comfortable in any situation. I had a willingness to engage on any topic and a curiosity about everything—all essential traits needed to develop and nurture a variety of relationships.

The word "producer" first registered with me when I saw *The Wizard of Oz* on television, right around the time my family moved to Los Angeles. We only had one black-and-white TV and my father surprised us with an invitation to watch the film at a friend's home so we could see it in color. I sat directly in front of the television, filled with anticipation. The music began and the dedication appeared: "For nearly forty years this story has given faithful service to the Young in Heart; and Time has been powerless to put its kindly philosophy out of fashion. To those of you who have been faithful to it in return . . . and to the Young in Heart . . . we dedicate this picture." I was young in heart and literally believed that this movie was made for people like me. The words "produced by Mervyn LeRoy" caught my attention; I thought the role of a producer was to make people happy.

David O. Selznick was another person who registered in my mind as a great producer. He specialized in taking great literature and adapting it for film. Not just his masterpiece *Gone with the Wind*, but *Rebecca, David Copperfield, Anna Karenina, The Prisoner of Zenda, The Adventures of Tom Sawyer,* and on and on. I discovered that the role of producer was demanding and multi-faceted after reading his book, *Memo from David O. Selznick.* I learned that in addition to finding the material, hiring the talent (writer, director, actors, etc.), and finding the money, a producer supervises every detail of production, post-production, and marketing. It seemed overwhelming to be a producer, but the example and success of Viva made the impossible seem possible. I wanted to learn.

I got my first break when Norman's secretary, Jadi Joe, heard that I had worked on Capitol Hill and asked me to back her up on the days she wasn't in the office. Jadi was first generation Chinese-American, grew up in Arkansas, had a hint of a Southern drawl, and one of the best laughs I'd ever heard. I looked up to her even though she was only a few years older than I. She made it possible for me to get the chance to take notes for Norman during run-throughs—the rehearsal held just before the first taping—and to transcribe his dictation, which was what I liked the most about the job. I found he had an amazing ability to simply sit down and dictate a funny scene that needed little revision. After I mentioned to him that I had been a theater major in college, he would occasionally ask me to read the many screenplays that were sent to him for his consideration. As time went by, he also asked me to attend dress rehearsals on the stage and give him my notes.

Norman was always open to hearing different points of view and feedback, even from a lowly receptionist, and I think he wanted me to have the experience of watching the rehearsals. I would notice where a line wasn't registering, or something like that—suggesting very small tweaks that might make a scene funnier. I loved the opportunity to go to the stage, sit where no one could see me, and watch these incredibly gifted people work to get a scene, a character, a moment just right. Norman had a closed-circuit TV in his office and watched the rehearsals from there. I'd meet with him after the rehearsals and give him my notes; over time, he trusted my instincts more and more. As implausible as it may seem, however, it was on the strength of my adventure in Washington, DC, when I had taken a break from college that would eventually elevate me from receptionist to Norman Lear's executive assistant.

In 1978, Norman decided to step away from his day-to-day activities supervising the shows to flex new creative muscles. No one, including me—and maybe even Norman—knew what that meant; but he had become exhausted from the demands on him and wanted to do something new. While discussions and meetings about who would assume his supervising responsibilities were ongoing, he read a small article in the *Los Angeles Times* that the Smithsonian Institution acquired the set from *The Muppet Show* for their pop culture collection. He wondered if the museum would also be interested in Archie and Edith Bunker's chairs from *All in the Family*.

One unremarkable day, he stood next to my desk and asked the head of marketing for Tandem (by then called Tandem/TAT), to call Kathy, and before he could get her last name out,

I said, "Yes?" He turned to me and asked, "Oh, Cathy, you worked in Washington, DC, do you know anyone connected to the Smithsonian?" It just so happened that I did. During my short time in DC, I had met John Brademas, a Democratic congressman from Indiana (who would later become the president of New York University). John was the majority whip in Congress, an important and powerful position, and a keen advocate for education and the arts. I also saw John as someone who knew how to make the impossible possible.

Brademas had spent his twenty-two years in Congress fighting for legislation to improve the lives of others in the arts, labor, education, health, and for young people with disabilities. I thought he would certainly know someone at the Smithsonian since he had co-sponsored the legislation for the creation of the National Endowment for the Arts and the National Endowment for the Humanities. Not only did he know who to call at the Smithsonian, but he also suggested we organize several events around the donation of the chairs, including a meeting with the president in the Oval Office, a reception in the Senate, a luncheon on Capitol Hill with members of Congress, and concluding with a late-night supper with the movers and shakers of Washington along with the principle cast of the series and Tandem/TAT's top executives. He graciously agreed to work with me on all of it. Shortly after my call with Brademas, I found myself trying to balance my role as receptionist and "new duties as assigned."

Norman saw the donation as a wonderful way to transition from the end of his tenure with *All in the Family* to his new role in the company. John put me in touch with Carl Scheele who worked in the Smithsonian's pop culture division. Over the next several months I worked closely with Carl on all the logistics of the donation and the related occasions. Events like these were common in Washington, DC, and Carl tried to temper my expectations about the number of acceptances we would have for the evening reception when the chairs would be officially donated. With that in mind, I sent out a "save the date" card for the event—and to Carl's surprise, ultimately more than a thousand people attended the reception held in the Hall of Flags in the National Museum of History and Technology.

I also reached out to Bob Squier, my old boss at the Democratic Convention, who had become one of the most successful political consultants in DC. When I asked if he could help get our cast and executives on President Carter's schedule, he agreed on one condition: He wanted a beer can from the bar Archie Bunker frequented. He got the can of beer and we got the meeting, but unfortunately the actor who played Archie, Carroll O'Connor, was unable to join us in DC due to health issues.

Today, it's common for celebrities to meet with the president of the United States, but it didn't happen often in the 1970s. There were no barricades around the White House; when we pulled up in front of the entrance, Sally Struthers, the actress who played Archie's daughter, Gloria, exited the limousine and shouted, "Honey, I'm home!" We all burst into laughter, which was a great way to enter the West Wing. When we were escorted into the Oval office, President and Mrs. Carter were extremely gracious and shook hands with everyone, but within minutes, chaos erupted as the doors to the portico opened and dozens of photographers rushed in. I stood off to the side next to someone from the White House communications office, and had trouble spelling the names of the cast and executives for the press to use, because everything happened so quickly.

After our meeting at the White House, we piled back into the cars and drove to Capitol Hill for a reception in a beautiful room just off the Senate side of the Capitol. California Senator Alan Cranston stood on the Senate floor and asked if he could

Oval Office, September 1978. Norman Lear shaking hands with President Carter with various family members and *All in the Family* cast looking on. Bette Davis in print dress with her back to the camera.

PHOTO COURTESY OF PRESIDENT CARTER LIBRARY COLLECTION

Edith and Archie Bunker's chairs on display
at the National Museum of American History
PHOTO BY WIKIPEDIA USER RADIOFAN (TALK)

interrupt remarks being given regarding President Carter's efforts with the Middle East Summit. Senator Cranston asked, "Will the senator from New York forgive me if I proceed very briefly on a totally extraneous matter?" New York Senator Daniel Patrick Moynihan replied, "Be happy to."

Senator Cranston began, "Mr. President, during this time of truly momentous historic development, it is not altogether unfitting that we pause briefly to take note of a less momentous but also, in its way, historic event. Tonight, in a special ceremony in the Hall of Flags in the National Museum of History and Technology, the Smithsonian Institution will

formally take possession for the ages of two distinctive arti-
facts of modern American culture: the chairs of Archie and
Edith Bunker . . . The Smithsonian has selected [the chairs] to
be preserved as part of the cultural legacy of our country."

Wisconsin Senator William Proxmire also spoke, and
summed up his view of *All in the Family*'s contribution,
"Although [the show] has brought a great deal of joy and laughter to millions of Americans, it has also done more to diminish
prejudice and bias, by getting people to laugh at the prejudices
we all hold, than almost any other action that has taken place in
the last 10 years." He added, "I think if we have made progress
since the great civil rights actions of 15 or 20 years ago in overcoming our biases, there is no activity that has done more to
accomplish it than this program, *All in the Family*."

The reception in the Senate was followed by a well-attended
luncheon on the House side with dozens of members. John
Brademas stood on the floor of the House and paid tribute to
the series: "Mr. Speaker, since January 12, 1971, when Archie
and Edith Bunker made their television debut, they and the
other characters of the much-honored television series, *All in
the Family*, have been weekly visitors in the home of millions
of Americans. Norman Lear who, as creator and producer of
the show, brought added dimensions to American humor and
broke new ground for American television."

The reception at the Smithsonian that night went off without a hitch except for one little snag that no one saw coming.
Dinah Shore, who had a very popular talk show at the time
and a career in films as an actress and singer throughout the
'40s and '50s, had called Norman immediately after she heard

that he was donating the chairs to the Smithsonian. She asked if she could bring her crew to DC and do a segment for her show during the ceremony. However, a week before the cast was to depart for DC, Ms. Shore called to say she was sick and asked whether it would be okay to substitute Bette Davis as her replacement. Who could say no to Bette Davis?

It did seem like an odd task for one of the greatest actresses of the Golden Age of Hollywood to substitute for a talk show host. If I had been excited to meet Orson Welles, I was elated to meet with Bette Davis in her suite at the Madison Hotel. As I reviewed all the logistics with her, I was surprised by how nervous she seemed. "I have never done a talk show before! I want to do this right!" She started to pace back and forth and lit up a cigarette. Before my eyes, she became Margo Channing in the classic film *All About Eve*.

We had built a temporary set at the Smithsonian that was close to the reception area so the cast could take turns being interviewed and then return to the event. However, Ms. Davis continued the interview with the entire cast plus Norman for almost an hour. Norman was irritated, but what could anyone do? Thankfully, in a hall filled with a thousand people, the invitees didn't seem to notice that Norman and the cast had disappeared. After the reception, several of the prominent movers and shakers of the town's political elite dined with the cast and executives at the private club Pisces. I gave up that late-night dinner where I would have sat next to Walter Cronkite because I couldn't bring myself to engage in even one more conversation. I was almost comatose; the fear that something might have gone wrong that day had drained me of all energy.

Carl Scheele made sure that the plaque for the display of the Bunker's chairs included a quote from "Dear Abby" (Abigail Van Buren) that read: "*All in the Family* has accomplished more about understanding America and what it's all about than any other show that's ever been on television." It was a great tribute to Norman and Bud, and the perfect time for Norman to transition to a new chapter in his life. The success of the events surrounding the donation to the Smithsonian definitely elevated my stature at Tandem/TAT. I had an opportunity to show what I could do if given the chance. All the training that I never thought of as training in the art of diplomacy, my mother's incessant urging to smile when in doubt, and observing my parents and their friends gave me a skill set I didn't know was a talent. Without realizing it, I had become a twenty-six-year-old woman who could work with powerful and talented people, see them as three-dimensional, and get something done. Norman gave me a photo, now faded, taken during our meeting with President and Mrs. Carter in the Oval office and wrote on it: "To Catherine who kicked ass to make this happen!"

Over the months leading up to the donation events in DC, Norman had moved his office to Century City to pursue his new endeavors. Alan Horn, the president of the company, had been chosen to supervise the TV series, so he relocated to Metromedia studios in Hollywood. Alan would go on to become one of the most respected executives in the entertainment industry. He would eventually become the president of 20th Century Fox, one of the co-founders of Castle Rock Entertainment (*A Few Good Men, When Harry Met Sally* . . .), the president and COO of Warner Bros (including supervising the *Harry Potter* series and *The Dark Knight* trilogy, among others), and chairman of Walt Disney Studios. Alan, too, was impressed with what I had accomplished in DC, and when he heard Norman was looking for an executive assistant, he recommended me for the position. Alan would continue to be an influence on my career in the most surprising and unexpected ways.

Norman had a gift for working with someone to help him find his sea legs when creating something new. I became that someone as he transitioned from television to wherever his new endeavors would take him. I didn't know what the position would entail, but I thought it was an exciting opportunity to be able to work directly with him. I quickly learned there were a few essential things I had to do: read everything, including newspapers, magazines, and bestselling books; see every movie; and stay in tune with what was happening around me—the joy, pain, frustrations, and the hopes and dreams emerging in our world. I was expected to always have conviction and a compelling argument for why a script, a book, or an idea was something worth pursuing. I had to be ready to answer Norman's daily unpredictable questions like, "What did you think of that op-ed in the [NY] *Times* today?"

My first assignment wasn't exactly what I expected. Norman had heard of a hypnotist, Mr. Fike, who'd had success helping people quit smoking. He made it possible for all the smokers in the office to work with the hypnotist, including me. The funniest part of the experience was the memo I sent out just before the sessions were to begin: "Mr. Fike has laryngitis so everyone gets one more week of smoking." That assignment was typically Norman. His interests ranged from the micro, like hiring a hypnotist to get people to quit smoking, to the macro, like launching an effort to fight the injustice he saw in the behaviors of people like televangelist Reverend James Bakker and his wife, Tammy Faye, with the long eyelashes and gushing tears.

It upset Norman to see these preachers on television take advantage of their audiences by making millions selling their products to well-meaning Christian viewers. He found the perfect vehicle for a film that would shine a light on opportunistic televangelists when he discovered a religious organization called the Universal Life Church (ULC). The unique concept behind ULC is that anyone can become a minister without the years of study required by other religious organizations. A minister in the Universal Life Church has all the rights and privileges afforded to clergy members of other faiths. Better yet, in 1974 a federal judge declared that ULC qualified for religious tax exemption. This meant that a ULC minister could declare expenses such as those for home, family, trips, and car as church related, so all such expenses could be written off, resulting in paying very little in taxes.

Reverend Kirby Hensley founded the ULC organization in 1959 and incorporated in 1962, with the first church service held in his Modesto, California, garage. Norman and I went to Modesto to meet with him and see for ourselves what Reverend Hensley did, and how the ordination worked. It appeared to be a very modest operation headquartered in a nondescript building with card tables set up in a large room. Checks were piled high from people who wanted to become ministers. All they had to do was send in twenty dollars to receive a certificate and follow several rules on how to set up their church.

Finally, I was going to be in the movie business. The film project would eventually be called *Religion*, and I was charged with identifying and interviewing people who had joined the ULC. My research included a trip to San Diego to meet with a tax lawyer, and to New York where I met two police officers who had figured out how to take advantage of the terrific tax incentives.

Norman loved the officers' story. Before joining the Universal Life Church, both were grossing about $22,000 a year, taking home $200 a week after taxes. Even with second jobs, they were still scraping by when they heard about the ULC from a police captain in the corrections department. The two officers did their due diligence and asked a lawyer to check out the organization. The lawyer came back and said, "If you comply with the rules and regulations, it's perfectly legal." That still didn't satisfy them, so they went to California and met with Reverend Hensley. They appreciated all that Hensley was doing and decided to trust him.

When the officers returned home and told their friends about it, they were met with laughter and derision, "You're going to go to jail!" That didn't stop them; one of the officers declared a converted garage behind his home a church, hanging a sign outside that read "Universal Life Church." He quickly started to conduct seminars. The other officer declared his home a church. Who was in his congregation and on the board of the Church? His wife, his mother, and himself. The only requirement, he told us, was that "you had to have strong beliefs, whatever that may be—there's only one religion and that's yourself."

My research on religion in America led me down some very interesting rabbit holes. I learned that the notion that "there's only one religion and that's yourself" wasn't too far removed from how early Americans viewed religion. In 1773, a young man named Jeremiah Moore landed in jail for preaching his views about Christianity without a license. In his own defense, Moore said, "God himself is the only one to whom man is accountable for his religious sentiments simply, nor has he erected any tribunal on earth qualified to judge whether the man worships in an acceptable manner or not." Moore eventually petitioned the Virginia Assembly demanding the right for Baptists to be free to worship without persecution. Thomas Jefferson was a member of the Virginia Assembly at the time and became his chief advocate. A few years later, James Madison, who authored the Bill of Rights, included these words in the First Amendment: "Congress shall make no law respecting an establishment of religion, or prohibiting the free exercise thereof . . ."

Hensley took that sentiment into the twentieth century and found a way to give individuals the same tax advantages as traditional churches. Like the Catholic Church, the Universal Life Church had churches all over the country, and donations to the churches were not sent back to the main church in Modesto, but deposited in banks closer to the satellite churches. The result was that if your home was that church, the board of that church decided how all donations were spent. In part, this is what people like Reverend James Baker and the two police officers were doing. Norman set up a meeting with Richard Pryor and Robin Williams to portray the officers in the film; one of the cops would "get religion," while the other would "get rich."

It was such a heady time to be in a meeting with these two legendary comedians one moment and then traveling to unexpected places to gather research for one of Norman's many projects, that I was taken aback when a friend asked about my career goals, "But what do you want to do?" I didn't understand the question. I was busy helping Norman achieve his goals, but my friend was insistent, "Yeah, but what are *your* goals?" It was a question I really didn't know how to answer. It turned out to be one of the most important questions anyone would ever ask me, because I had to stop and think, What are my goals? I thought my primary objective was to do a good job as Norman's executive assistant and hadn't thought much beyond that. I dreamed of being a producer, but didn't know how I would actually become one.

Norman was a writer/producer, which means he always wrote the material he produced for television or film. I wasn't a screenwriter, so I was unsure how a non-writer became a producer. There was something else that was hard to articulate then, but easier now. The notion of equality in the workplace was just starting to be defined. There were all sorts of attitudes and workplace behaviors—like men commenting on a woman's appearance, or the view that a job opportunity had to go to a man because he had a family to support—that only reinforced that women in leadership roles weren't taken seriously.

I certainly evolved in my thinking over time, but when I was twenty-six years old in 1978, it took my friend's question to force me to take my first adult step on the road to becoming a warrior. I had to say out loud what was worth fighting for and told this friend about my dream to get *A Wrinkle in Time* made into a movie. I asked him to read the book, fully expecting he wouldn't like it and would try to convince me to put away my childish dream. His reaction was the opposite; he loved it and saw the story as a cross between *Star Wars* and *The Wizard of Oz*. His response gave me the courage to ask Norman to read it. I had confidence in my compelling belief for why *Wrinkle* should be made into a film.

About a week after I gave Norman the book, I ran into him in the hallway and asked him about the movie *Hair*. He had just been to a screening of the film, and I was eager to know what he thought. He said, "It was really visionary—the director, Miloš Forman, had a real vision, just like that book you like so much. It needs a visionary to make it work, but I don't see it as something for me to write or direct." Without a moment's hesitation, I asked, "Can I go after the film rights, anyway?" I knew that the company had to have an exclusive agreement with the author to begin developing the book into film. He thought for a second and then said, "Yes, if Alan Horn approves." Within a day, Alan Horn had a copy of *A Wrinkle in Time* on his desk.

While I waited for Alan to read the book, Norman's concerns about the evangelists' messages on TV grew more serious. It was the Reverend Jimmy Swaggart's plea for "good Christians" to remove a US Supreme Court justice that he had found especially galling. According to Swaggart, there were *good* and *bad* Christians, depending on their political points of view. Norman respected and admired the long tradition in Christianity of inclusion, tolerance, forgiveness, acceptance, and love. This more intolerant view of Christianity wasn't his main issue with the TV preachers, however; it was their use of radio and television as a means to amplify the message that America was solely a Christian nation. He found it terrifying if that belief were to be embraced and spread on a wider scale. At that time, it had only been thirty years since Norman risked his life fighting Nazis so that America would continue to be the land of the free.

The televangelists' mischaracterization of Christianity bothered me as well. My entire upbringing was that the church was about love in thought, word, and deed. If Christianity was political, I thought it was to practice the Golden Rule in all things: "Do unto others as you would have others do unto you"—not as a litmus test about who was a good or bad Christian. I had been raised an Episcopalian, and my mother said that when I was about five years old I would wake her up so we wouldn't be late for church. In fourth grade, I wanted desperately to be in the youth choir even though I couldn't sing. I wanted to wear the long red robes with the little cap on my head and join the procession into the main church on special occasions. The choirmaster was a kind man who agreed to let me join if I only mouthed the words to the hymns. I was in seventh heaven.

My first encounter with any controversy regarding Christianity was in high school. I was devastated when my high school boyfriend told me that his mother no longer wanted us to date because we were of different religious faiths. Beverly Hills High School had a large population of students who were Jewish and I thought that since Jesus was Jewish, being a Christian just meant an "and"—Jewish *and* Christian. Up until that moment, I wasn't fully aware that religious differences had the potential to divide people.

Jerry Falwell, another minister I had been researching, also divided people into good and bad when he created the political action group Moral Majority. Falwell, despite being a newcomer to politics, was a big believer in the "good" Christian point of view on a broad range of political issues. I learned from my research that Falwell was a product of a subculture that sprang up after the 1925 *Scopes* trial. That trial set in motion all that we see in the political/social/religious unrest today. Williams Jennings Bryan, a conservative congressman from Nebraska, represented the state of Tennessee in a lawsuit brought against John Scopes, a high school biology teacher who taught Charles Darwin's theory of evolution. Clarence Darrow, a well-respected civil rights lawyer from Chicago, represented Scopes.

The consequences of the lawsuit were bigger than anyone anticipated. It pitted those who believed in the literal interpretation of the Bible against those who saw it as a book inspired by God and filled with stories that weren't literally true, but provided guidance on how to lead a moral life. Ultimately, the judge ruled in favor of Bryan's literal interpretation, preventing the theory of evolution from being taught in Tennessee public schools. However, the public felt Darrow had won the argument. From that moment on, those who thought that every word in the Bible was literally true were considered backwards in their thinking. The 1960 film *Inherit the Wind* directed by Stanley Kramer brilliantly dramatizes the heated moment of that trial.

In response, the fundamentalists—those who advocate strict conformity to biblical literalism—created their own churches and schools, mostly in the South. Reverend Jerry Falwell was a pastor at the Thomas Road Baptist Church in Lynchburg, Virginia. Falwell was apolitical until Reverend Thomas Schaeffer came into his life in the late 1970s. Schaeffer was also an American fundamentalist preacher who was concerned that the "consensus of our society no longer rests upon a Christian basis but upon a humanistic one. Humanism is man putting himself at the center of all things, rather than the creator God." Secular humanists became the devil in all things.

I had never even heard the words "secular humanist" until I started doing research for Norman's film *Religion*. Schaeffer was the one who pushed fundamentalists to oppose abortion and encouraged Jerry Falwell to get more politically involved, leading to the creation of the Moral Majority. As Norman continued to watch and listen to what Falwell preached, he became more and more worried. He knew better than anyone about the power and reach of television and began to think that producing a film wasn't enough—it might take two years to get one to the screen, and he would likely miss the moment to counter this divisive message.

One morning, he arrived at the office with a few pages of a script he had written the night before. I don't even think he knew what he was going to do with it, but I told him the tone was really angry. I used an expression my grandmother always said, "You get more flies with honey than vinegar." He agreed and revised it to sound more like Archie Bunker as a man troubled about the literature he was receiving in the mail. The script read:

Hi. I have a problem. I'm religious. We're a religious family, but that don't mean we see things the same way politically. Now, here come certain preachers on radio and TV and in the mail, telling us on a bunch of political issues that there's just one Christian position, and implying if we don't agree we're not good Christians.

So, my son is a bad Christian on two issues. My wife is a good Christian on those issues but she's a bad Christian on two others. Lucky me, I'm a hundred percent Christian because I agree with the preacher on all of them. Now, my problem is I know my boy is as good Christian as me. My wife, she's better. So maybe there's something wrong when people, even preachers, suggest that other people are good Christians or bad Christians depending on their political views. That's not the American Way."

Norman decided to turn the script into 30- and 60-second ads with non-actors talking directly to the camera. The leadership at Tandem/TAT was wary that Norman wanted to take on the Christian conservative movement alone, and he understood.

While ongoing conversations were held to explore how to find other concerned citizens that may have held similar views, Alan Horn sent me a note that said he had read *Wrinkle* and liked it—and told me to "Go for it."

I now had the go-ahead to track down Madeleine L'Engle's agent through her publisher, Farrar, Straus and Giroux, to inquire if the film rights were available. I also read on the book's back cover that Madeleine lived in New York City and quickly searched our office for a copy of the Manhattan white pages (in pre-internet times it's how phone numbers and addresses were listed). I found one hidden under a pile of papers on top of a metal filing cabinet and didn't hesitate to send a letter this time.

I remembered how hesitant I had been about sending Walt Disney that letter, and about knocking on Katharine Hepburn's door—but not this time. I discovered that Madeleine L'Engle's married name was Franklin and thought it proper to begin the letter, "Dear Ms. Franklin." My letter read:

> The beauty, grace and vision of your work *A Wrinkle in Time* has remained with me since I first read the book fifteen years ago. Often, I have thought about the need for its scope and magic to be brought to the public as a motion picture. At present I am working with Norman

Lear who has read your book at my suggestion. He
agrees that the heroic adventures of Meg and Charles
Wallace would make an exquisite film.

I finished by asking if we could meet in New York City to
discuss a film option on the book. Back in the day, long distance calls were expensive to make so I included in the letter,
"Please feel free to call collect." About a week later, the phone
rang in my office and the operator asked, "Will you accept a
collect call from Madeleine L'Engle?"

3
Working with Warriors

The spirit of liberty is the spirit that seeks to
understand the minds of other men and women.

JUDGE LEARNED HAND

A s I sat across from Madeleine L'Engle that day atop the World Trade Center, I was reminded of the great female movie stars that had mesmerized me in my childhood; she looked and sounded just like one of them. I was awe-struck not only because she wrote *A Wrinkle in Time*, but her stature reminded me of Rosalind Russell in *His Girl Friday*. Madeleine spoke with the Mid-Atlantic accent common in 1940s films—a blend of American and British English accents—she didn't look or sound like anyone I had ever met. I didn't know it at that time, but I was sitting across from the woman who would become my lifelong mentor—and I had been sent there by another mentor confident that I would succeed.

My mind raced as we ordered lunch while I tried to find the words that would convince her to trust me. She made it that much harder when she mentioned that over the years hundreds of people had approached her for the film rights, but she had always said no. "No one will agree to a clause that you can't change character or theme," she shrugged. How was I going to outdo those hundreds who had already asked about the rights? My strategy was to speak from the heart since it was all I knew how to do. I began with how the book came into my life.

I told her how reluctant I had been to read the book, but then fell in love with it the moment I read that Meg was trying to get rid of her faults. I told her that my view of God had been influenced greatly by her depiction of a universe where love was more important than any one religion. I also mentioned how the book helped me when Kennedy was assassinated to grasp that darkness does exist and can be overcome. Madeleine understood this. The book had been the most borrowed book in school libraries during those dark days—it gave many young people a sense of hope and courage. She was also pleased that I understood how integral to the story it was for Meg to return alone to the evil planet Camazotz to rescue her younger brother. It was revelatory in 1963 to think that a young girl could do something her father couldn't, and his trust in her ability to succeed was crucial. I also mentioned my almost-sent letter to Walt Disney and my childhood dream to make and star in the movie, which made her laugh. Something indescribable happened between the two of us that day. By the time we were in the taxi on our drive uptown, Madeleine turned and said, "Let's see how we can make this happen."

On my way back to LA, I stopped in New Mexico to visit a friend, Michael Hurd, who lived on a ranch of 2,300 acres just

Henriette Wyeth unfinished portrait, March 1979

outside of Roswell. Michael was then, and is still, a talented artist who comes from a family of artists. His mother was Henriette Wyeth (N. C. Wyeth's daughter and sister to Andrew Wyeth), and his father was the western water colorist Peter Hurd. One morning while I was there, Henriette said she would like to paint my portrait. I was very flattered that she asked, since she had painted the official White House portrait of Patricia Nixon and is considered one of the great female artists of the twentieth century. Henriette told engaging stories and had piercing eyes that could see right through you. The portrait has always held special significance for me because it is such a marker for who I was the week I first met Madeleine L'Engle. I couldn't stay at the ranch long enough for her to complete the portrait, which seems fitting in retrospect since I was unfinished, still evolving into the woman I would become.

Once I was back in California, it seemed like the deal with Madeleine wasn't going to close. Six months passed with lawyers going back and forth—and it all came down to that troublesome clause about not changing character or theme. Most companies saw this as a deal-breaker, because they want the freedom to do whatever they want with the material—they could conceivably go so far as to throw everything out but the title. I made a compelling argument to Norman that the characters and themes were the reason we wanted to option the book. He agreed and ruled to move forward; the company accepted the clause, and the deal was signed.

Aljean Harmetz, a writer for the *New York Times*, contacted us after the project was announced and wrote a story about our plans for the film. As soon as the story ran in the *Times*, we started receiving letters from *Wrinkle* fans across the country, and I discovered how popular the book had grown since I first read it. People, young and old, would stop Norman constantly wherever he went and tell him about their special fondness for the book. We had no specific timeframe, other than wanting to make the movie as soon as it was feasible. Four studios were interested in working with us, but we wanted to develop the screenplay ourselves and perhaps finance the film too. While Norman's film *Religion* had been placed on the back burner as we put our efforts into understanding the issues surrounding the rise of the religious right, the film adaption of *A Wrinkle in Time* remained one of our top priorities.

In October 1979, I had my first official meeting with Madeleine at the library of the Cathedral of St. John the Divine in New York City where she was the resident librarian. The first thing I noticed as I entered the room were the high ceilings, the large window facing a beautiful garden with trees that had started to change color, and that sweet musky smell of old books. We sat at a long wooden table and I could feel the well-worn scratches under my fingertips. It was a dream come true to sit and talk with Madeleine about Meg and her journey. It was the first time after convincing her about my love for *Wrinkle* that I heard Madeleine talk about the book. I was a little taken aback when I began to hear this wasn't just a child's adventure story, but Madeleine's search for meaning written at a very difficult time in her life. I realized this undertaking was far more than I had expected.

Working with Norman meant that I was constantly juggling a variety of projects that weren't only entertainment focused. Upon my return to LA, *Wrinkle* was set aside while I concentrated on finding like-minded individuals who shared Norman's concern about the religious right. Because there was no internet, I spent hours reading through magazines for interviews given by anyone who touched on the topic, researching religious leaders of all faiths. Norman was also focused on another project he wanted to pursue: a series of political debates with the candidates then running for president in 1980. The format would be fashioned after the concept of a matador and his picadors. The picadors were to spar with "the bull" to get the audience excited about the matador's confrontation with the bull. Both former Governor Ronald Reagan and Vice President Walter Mondale were interested in participating. The first issue under discussion was to be the controversial Panama Canal Treaty. I was sent to DC in late spring to meet with Senator Jake Garn's staff about another possible issue: the SALT II Treaty (Strategic Arms Limitation Talks).

While in town, I stopped by the office of Senator Mike Gravel from Alaska who had hired me during the break I had taken between my junior and senior years of college. Mike Gravel was a risk taker from an early age. Following his service in the Army's Counter Intelligence Corps in Europe, he earned a degree in economics from Columbia University, supporting himself driving a taxi in New York City. After evaluating where a young man with no money might fulfill a dream of becoming a US senator, he set out for Alaska in 1956—before Alaska became a state in 1959.

Senators who don't toe the party line often get labeled a "maverick," and Senator Gravel was definitely a maverick. He entered 4,000 pages of the Pentagon Papers into the Congressional Record just before the US Supreme Court lifted an injunction on publishing them. He was also opposed to any new construction of nuclear power plants and the continuation of the Vietnam War, and he filibustered to end the draft. Gravel was courageous for questioning the status quo and progressive in his beliefs. He was also a very encouraging and a supportive mentor.

My time on the Hill in 1973–1974, watching and observing the art of politics, taught me more than I could ever have learned sitting in a classroom. There were two moments that have stayed with me. The first was standing outside the White House on August 9, 1974, the day Richard Nixon resigned. The evening air was thick with humidity as I stood beside hundreds of others there to mark the peaceful transition of power between Nixon and Ford. My faith in our political system had been rocked by the Watergate scandal, and now it was restored. Justice had been done. I was there that night as a witness to history and have carried that feeling that the good guys can win for the rest of my life.

The other moment that left a lasting impact was attending a meeting Senator Gravel had with the legendary Senator Russell Long from Louisiana and William Simon, then secretary of the treasury. The meeting took place in one of those ornate rooms on the Senate side of the Capitol, and I had been asked to sit in on the meeting to take notes. For thirty minutes, the three men traded lively and engaging stories and each tried to one-up the other. They never talked about the issue on the table until the last three minutes of the meeting when a decision was reached and agreed upon. I was confused; I thought they had wasted precious time telling stories. Later, Senator Gravel helped me understand that the trading of stories was all about establishing trust. They needed to trust one another before coming to an agreement.

It was an invaluable lesson about the need to cultivate trust to work effectively with others and that things aren't always what they seem. After that experience, I knew the importance of engaging on all sorts of topics with whomever I was working—not just the central topic of discussion. That's probably why I brought up my research on Jerry Falwell and the Moral Majority while catching up with old friends in Gravel's office. Within minutes, Donna Harlow, a senior member of Gravel's team who had taken me under her wing during my time on the Hill, blurted out, "Jerry Falwell? You should see this."

It was a letter to senators and congressmen from Dr. Charles Bergstrom, a Lutheran minister who was very concerned about the threat the Moral Majority posed to the separation of church and state. I tracked down Dr. Bergstrom and discovered that he shared all of Norman's concerns. He gave me a copy of his letter to take back to Los Angeles as proof that we were not alone in our fears about the religious right.

In the fall of 1979, so many things were happening at once. We were building a list of like-minded people to develop a wagon train of sorts around Norman. As he took on the televangelists, I began working with Madeleine, and in December, I learned that I would soon be on Ronald Reagan's presidential campaign bus and plane. Norman had read an interview Reagan had given to the *Los Angeles Times* and thought it would be great to get that kind of interview with Reagan on camera with the idea of turning the footage into a documentary. Norman believed Reagan was going to be a real force in national politics. He approached Bob Scheer, a well-respected *LA Times* journalist, with the idea and Scheer loved it.

My task was to hire a very small crew (sound and camera men) and accompany Bob to coordinate the logistics for his interview with Reagan. Being part of the press corps on a presidential campaign was unlike anything I had ever done. It was interesting to observe how much the press swapped stories about what they were seeing and hearing, then competed for time with the candidate, campaign volunteers, and supporters in the crowd. Those crowds that would show up at a campaign stop could be fairly large or just a dozen or so people. Then, there was the food on the campaign trail. No matter where we went, we knew to eat as much as possible because we never knew when we would eat again. Our time was definitely not our own—everything revolved around the candidate's schedule.

That schedule was intense. We arrived in Birmingham, Alabama, on February 21, 1980, at seven fifteen in the morning and by two in the afternoon we departed for Orlando, Florida. The next day we drove to Palm Beach and Boca Raton, and that afternoon flew to Augusta, Georgia, eventually arriving in Manchester, New Hampshire, later that night—three states and six cities in two days. We stayed with the press bus as Reagan toured New Hampshire. The state was crucial to Reagan at that point in the campaign. He had done poorly in the Iowa caucuses a month before and desperately needed to win New Hampshire. On February 27, we arrived in Boston and flew with the Reagan entourage to Columbia, South Carolina.

It was on the flight from Boston to Columbia that Scheer conducted an extraordinary interview with Reagan, who was utterly charming and gracious. Over the heavy background noise from the jet engine, they chatted together like long lost friends discussing a range of issues, including abortion. Reagan turned to Bob and said, "I don't think it will win me the election but I feel [abortion] is wrong and that's all I can say about the subject. I understand other people see it differently. I understand this will not help me win the election, but that's how I feel." That opinion probably helped him win the election, but neither the documentary nor the series of political debates ever got made—the networks thought they were "too political." Decades later, Norman donated the interview footage to the Ronald Reagan Presidential Library.

I mention the Reagan story because of another important connection I made, completely unrelated to the 1980 presidential campaign. In my search for a film crew, I reached out to a friend of mine, David Hoffman, who was a very successful independent filmmaker I met while working for Senator Gravel. Over the course of our phone conversation, he asked what else I was doing and I mentioned my research on the Moral Majority. He said, "Moral Majority? You need to speak with my good friends Sandy Slater and Marc Porat."

Sandy was also an independent film producer who had worked on several films with David. At the time, her father, Joe Slater, was the president of an organization called the

Aspen Institute. A conference was held each summer in Aspen, Colorado, that became a forerunner to organizations like TED Talks and the Allen Conference in Sun Valley. Among the people gathered that summer were several who shared their concerns about the threat to civil liberties posed by groups like the Moral Majority. The threat was not that religious leaders didn't have a right to their views; it was the amplification of their views on such a broad scale using television and radio. It was important to offer an alternative message: Your political views didn't make you a good or bad Christian, America isn't a Christian nation, and our fundamental promise of liberty and justice for all allows for a more open and tolerant society.

Both Sandy and Marc had met a number of individuals who were aware and concerned of the impact Jerry Falwell was having with his TV show, *Old Time Gospel Hour*. I met with them in New York and we quickly discovered that we were kindred spirits. It was clear to us that we needed to bring Norman together with those they had met that summer in Aspen. Sandy and Marc introduced Norman to Jim Autry, a publishing executive who had been at the Aspen Institute that summer and was then the chief executive officer of the Meredith Publishing Corporation. Jim introduced Norman to other people with the same concerns about the religious right, and bit by bit we met with an impressive assortment of religious and business leaders, requiring Norman and me to often be on the road to bring these people together.

We travelled across the country and met in restaurants, living rooms, and offices with people in Iowa, Illinois, Indiana,

Ohio, Maryland, Virginia, California, and New York. In Indiana, we met with Father Ted Hesburgh, who had been president of Notre Dame University for thirty-five years. In Chicago, Illinois, we met with Dr. Martin Marty, one of the most well-regarded religious historians in the country. In Iowa, we met with Senator Harold Hughes, a devout Christian and former governor of the state. We met with successful business leaders such as Andrew Heiskell, who was then chairman and CEO of Time, Inc., and David Rockefeller, then chairman and CEO of Chase Manhattan Bank—and dozens more like them who agreed to join our effort. Everyone was concerned about the religious right and committed to raising awareness about it in their respective communities.

To get advice on how best to launch the TV ads that Norman had written, we met with a political media legend, Tony Schwartz. Tony had created hundreds of commercials for corporations, designed sound for a number of Broadway shows and produced television and radio commercials for presidential campaigns. Once again, my friend David Hoffman, who had worked with Tony on several of his corporate projects, urged us to meet with him. Tony was considered the best at strategizing a media campaign, and that was what Norman's ads were becoming—a media campaign to counter the televangelists.

The first thing Tony asked was whether we had done any research on the impact of the religious right; the answer was no. Norman just had a gut feeling as a successful television producer and civil liberties advocate that the messaging of the religious right was divisive and a threat to our sense of pluralism and diversity. He hadn't wanted to take the time to do research; he wanted to act immediately. Tony was impressed with Norman's commitment, which made him all the more willing to help. He asked us if we were doing the ad for some group or organization, but we hadn't thought that far ahead, and replied that we were in the process of forming such a group. Then Tony asked the $64,000 question: Does the organization have a name?

Norman wanted to take back the phrases and American symbols that the conservative movement had long claimed as theirs. In Tony's office, after a few minutes of tossing out possibilities, the words "People for the American Way" came together for the first time. An hour later, while jogging down a street in New York in three-inch high heels to keep up with Norman's quick pace, I said, "People for the American Way, People For . . . it could work!" We were the first two members of People For and the ads would now end with "sponsored by People For the American Way." We turned to Norman's daughter Ellen, who was then a graphic designer, to create a logo and we soon felt official—a name and a logo.

Learning to network and connect with like-minded individuals with common interests was one of the great takeaways from my time working with Norman. His notion of flexing new creative muscles was vast and grew to encompass politics, movies, television, philanthropy, and business decisions that impacted the company. I worked closely with him on identifying and meeting with potential allies, helped to raise funds for the effort, and assisted in supervising the production of our public service announcements. I was the primary person entrusted to implement his interests—"the invisible glue that

With Norman Lear, circa 1980
REPRODUCED BY PERMISSION FROM NORMAN LEAR

makes things happen," as he said. But no matter where I was sent, or what new project was on the horizon, I never let my desire to adapt *A Wrinkle in Time* for the screen fall through the proverbial crack.

The question Norman and I continued to discuss was whether to approach a writer or a director first. As I made lists of possibilities, Norman grew more convinced that the best visionary director for *Wrinkle* was Stanley Kubrick (*Spartacus, 2001: A Space Odyssey*). No one could better capture the mystery and spectacle inherent in the story and make it the big cosmic adventure that we envisioned. In December 1979, we met with John Calley, a very thoughtful man who was a beloved film executive and close to Kubrick. Calley loved the book and agreed to get Kubrick to read it. A month later, word got back to us that Kubrick liked *Wrinkle*, but other projects were calling him in a different direction.

I didn't have time to be too disappointed—our efforts to counter the Moral Majority and other similar groups had kicked into high gear. We knew we wanted to keep the effort nonpartisan and to make sure this network we were building was composed of both Democrats and Republicans, as well as people from different faiths. One meeting that left a lasting impression was our visit with Dr. Hudson Armerding, the president of Wheaton College, considered the Harvard of Christian colleges. We thought Dr. Armerding might wish to join our effort, but realized walking around the campus that day how naïve we were. While Dr. Armerding felt that change in behavior came through prayer, the students we spoke with thought change in behavior came through new laws that better reflected their conservative beliefs. Listening to this new generation of Christian students, I was taken aback by their embrace of a God that seemed so narrow in scope.

Many years later, I was reminded of that day in Wheaton when I read Sarah Arthur's book *A Light So Lovely*, an insightful exploration of Madeleine L'Engle's spiritual legacy. Sarah was a young student at Wheaton in the 1990s and shared similar observations in her introduction. She wrote: ". . . I arrived at Wheaton where I encountered a small but vocal subset of students who insisted that the "things of the world" and "the things of God" were divided into strict binary categories. And God only worked through the latter. Thus, we could only believe this *or* that; only creation *or* evolution, only faith *or* science, only fact *or* fiction, only sacred *or* secular, only conservative *or* liberal, only Scripture *or* nothing, only, only, only. For the first time in my life I was being told—continually, fervently, bluntly—what God can't do."

Norman advocated for our Founding Fathers' vision of a more inclusive America, which is what resonated with those who joined our effort. Our statement of purpose read:

> In times of hardship, in times of crises, societies
> throughout history have experienced wrenching
> dislocations in their fundamental values and beliefs.
> The decades of the Eighties and Nineties will be
> troubled times—some predict the most turbulent
> since the 1930s—and we are alarmed that some
> current voices of stridency and division may replace
> those of reason and unity. If these voices continue
> unchallenged, the results will be predictable: an
> increase in tension among races, classes and religions,
> a rise in "demonology" and hostility, a breakdown in
> community and social spirit, a deterioration of free and
> open dialogue and the temptation to grasp at simplistic
> solutions for complex problems.
>
> People For the American Way was established
> to address these matters. Our purpose is to meet
> the challenges of discord and fragmentation with
> an affirmation of "The American Way." By this we
> mean pluralism, individuality, freedom of thought,
> expression and religion, a sense of community, and

tolerance and compassion for others. We stand for values and principle, not for single issues, chosen candidates, or partisan causes. People For the American Way will reach out to all Americans and affirm that in our society, the individual still matters; that there is reason to believe in the future—not to despair of it—and we must strengthen the common cords that connect us as humans and as citizens.

That mission statement reflects the ideas Norman referred to in all our meetings. He was prescient in his warning about the changes taking place in America and that continue to this day. He genuinely cared about the people we met across the country, especially the religious scholars. I, too, was impressed with their intellect and deeply held beliefs. Everyone mattered as far as Norman was concerned, which was why he was so fierce in his fight for diversity and pluralism—the very foundation of The American Way. I found myself caught up in his passion to counter the divisive voices decrying pluralism and diversity and was committed to implementing his vision. My goal to produce films seemed like it was far off in the distance, but it wasn't—I was just going at it sideways.

I had thought being a producer meant meetings with writers, directors, studio heads; being on a sound stage, in the editing room; and conducting marketing discussions on how to sell the film. But Norman taught me there was a crucial step that had to be taken before any of that: Know your audience. He came to realize just how important this was after writing and producing his 1971 film, *Cold Turkey*, starring Dick Van

Dyke and Bob Newhart. It was primarily shot in Greenfield, Iowa, and had a funny premise—a tobacco company offers to award $25 million to any town that can quit smoking for thirty days. The tobacco company wanted to prove that no one could quit cold turkey, but the fictional town of Eagle Rock, Iowa, led by Reverend Clayton Brooks played by Dick Van Dyke, accepts the challenge. The company, worried that the town might succeed, sends their PR man, played by Bob Newhart, to sabotage their efforts. After overcoming incredible odds in some hilarious situations, the town wins the challenge.

Meeting and working in Iowa gave Norman insight into the mindset of people living in the Midwest that proved quite helpful in his later conversations with the network during the early days of *All in the Family*. The executives would argue that "No one in Iowa would want to see this," and Norman could say with tremendous self-confidence, "Oh, yes they do!" He knew his audience, and that gave him strong convictions and the willingness to defy the network's attempt at censure. I learned this same lesson on the road while creating People For the American Way. I wasn't on a sound stage, but I was getting to know the audience for *A Wrinkle in Time* and how much the book meant to people from every age and walk of life.

Everyone who had read it seemed to have a different lens through which they viewed the book. My ongoing task was to find the perfect blend of book and film without losing Madeleine's unique vision. For many readers, *Wrinkle* gave them a view of the universe they had never imagined, but the most common refrain I heard was, "There are no words to describe what the book has meant to me." One person burst into tears just talking about her feelings for it. The one constant was that the story continued to hold a special place in the hearts of fans long after they had left childhood. Their responses continued to inspire me to stay the course to get it made, especially when I would run into roadblock after roadblock in the years ahead.

After Stanley Kubrick passed on the project and our attention turned to all things "People For," I raised the idea of adapting *Wrinkle* as a Broadway musical. Norman was intrigued and suggested we discuss the idea with Sam Cohn, a legendary super-agent. Sam was one of the co-founders of the talent agency ICM, and in the 1970s and '80s he represented just about anybody who was somebody in film and in theater—including Meryl Streep, Mike Nichols, Robin Williams, Paul Newman, Whoopi Goldberg, and so many others. He was based in New York and known to rarely return phone calls. Luckily for us, he returned Norman's call, and we met for lunch at his daily hang out, the Russian Tea Room in New York City.

The Russian Tea Room is next to Carnegie Hall and doesn't look like much on the outside, but once you cross the threshold you are taken back in time. It has an Old World feel of elegance and glamour, its deep red leather booths providing privacy for all the meetings that have taken place there over the years. There are a few tables in the center of the room, and that is where we sat. I thought that Sam most likely wanted everyone who entered the restaurant to see him meeting with Norman Lear—which was fine with me, because I wanted to see everyone who entered the restaurant.

I practically had another out-of-body experience sitting at a table in the iconic Russian Tea Room with Norman Lear and Sam Cohn discussing *A Wrinkle in Time* as a possible Broadway musical. At one point during the discussion, Norman left the table to make a call (cell phones not invented in those days) and Sam continued to engage in conversation with me. He said, "You know, when Norman and Bud Yorkin became partners, it was Bud who was the famous one." I never knew how successful Bud had been before their partnership began; it was eye-opening to think of Norman as a struggling writer.

While I hadn't known Norman during that earlier period of his life, I had certainly heard a number of stories about his time working with Jerry Lewis and Tennessee Ernie Ford, and the movies he and Bud produced. Norman had good reason to feel extremely confident in all he had accomplished, and yet I saw his moments of doubt on all his projects, questioning whether we were going in the right direction. So often we were creating something new, unable to predict the outcome of any meeting. I saw that mix of self-doubt and determination to move forward as essential ingredients for what it took to succeed. Walt Disney said it best, "Get a good idea and stay with it. Dog it, and work at it until it's done right."

Having confidence about what you are pursuing takes courage—and Norman had that in spades despite his moments of uncertainty. When I lacked self-confidence, he would urge me to focus on *why* I was in the room—what it was that I hoped to accomplish—and my confidence would grow as I focused on that *why*. It would take me years to feel confident in all situations, but observing and listening to him made it seem possible. Exploring the idea of a Broadway musical was just one more example of him taking a risk and asking the question—what if? We ultimately concluded that a stage adaptation about three young children would be too difficult to accomplish, and dropped the idea.

The decision disappointed me, but what I didn't understand at the time was how much I was learning from taking wrong turns as much as from taking the right ones. It wasn't just Norman who was flexing new creative muscles; I was learning that I had creative muscles to flex, and talents that I didn't recognize as talents. I had to constantly juggle a multitude of projects and the responsibilities on my plate grew as Norman's interests grew. As a way of coping with all that was expected of me, I found great inspiration in Norman's approach to life. He would say, "You can go through life two ways: trusting or wary. You may get hurt more if you go through trusting, but you won't miss any of the action." And this: "Life is like a carousel; the joy is in reaching for the brass ring not just in getting it." I worked to find the joy in reaching for the brass ring, which is why setbacks didn't set me back. I was like a sponge in my late twenties—soaking up everything around me and very trusting.

One project in particular, *Heartsounds*, based on the book by the same title provided great opportunities for me to learn from others. Fay Kanin was hired to write the script and she had marvelous stories from her illustrious career in movies and television. While working on that project, I met ABC executive Brandon Stoddard who had been responsible for the megahit *Roots*. He later went on to become the president of ABC Entertainment. Swapping war stories at the start of any meeting happened as often in show business as it did in politics—only the stories seemed more glamorous. Brandon had great stories. My favorite was the time he met Katharine Hepburn, Laurence Olivier, and the venerable director George Cukor on the set of the ABC special *Love Among the Ruins*. He said, "I'm standing there facing these three legends and didn't know what to say." I loved hearing that even Brandon had moments where he, too, felt awkward in the presence of such megastars.

The person who consistently amazed me with an unerring sense of true excellence was Norman. Every morning he would come to the office with a piece of paper—and often several tiny pieces of paper—with his jotted notes listing things to get done that day. His range of interests seemed boundless. His ideas could be inspired by last night's dinner conversation, by a book he was reading, or by something overheard in the elevator on his way into the office.

We would also meet with a parade of fascinating people seeking his advice or support for one reason or another. Muhammad Ali met with us to discuss Ali's possible participation in a People For ad, and he not only brought his own personal photographer but a small suitcase of magic tricks. It was surreal to watch the former heavyweight champion of the world demonstrating a version of the shell game. Another time, a reporter from The Washington Post met with Norman to discuss an issue and brought along twenty-one-year-old John F. Kennedy Jr. I've not met anyone since who had such an infectious and radiant smile. Maria Shriver came to visit with her boyfriend, a shy bodybuilder named Arnold Schwarzenegger, who waited out in the lobby.

The downside to my time working with Norman was that I had no personal life. He wasn't an average writer, producer, or boss. I spent my every waking moment thinking about how to keep up with him. In 1980, a national survey was conducted about entertainment and entertainers, and one of the questions was, "Who is the most well-known name in entertainment: George Lucas, Francis Coppola, or Norman Lear?" Most answered Norman Lear, which surprised me. Norman was more famous than George Lucas? But both conservatives and liberals liked him; he had the brilliant ability to poke fun at the human condition, and everyone could use a reality check now and then. Conservatives loved the way Archie made fun of his liberal son-in-law Mike Stivic, and liberals loved that Norman made fun of Archie's conservative views.

Norman taught me, and so many others, to believe in the impossible. Anyone who came to him for advice was made to feel like their project had a chance. He had a prodigious ability to take a good idea and make it great. He really did believe that life was like a carousel and the joy was found in the reaching for the brass ring not just in getting it. He also had a knack for hearing an idea and using it as a launching pad to another idea—with no particular rhyme or reason, but it was often a terrific new direction. This is how the idea to produce the ABC TV special called *I Love Liberty* came to be.

Before we found a writer for *Wrinkle* we had many thought-provoking conversations sitting around his conference table. We had ongoing discussions about the book's characters, themes, and what we hoped to achieve. It was in one of those conversations that Norman stood up and said, "That's it." "What?" I asked. "Young people need to have reason for hope and faith in the future. They need to experience what defines this country." He envisioned a television special that presented a great big love letter to America with celebrities, stories about the American experiment, and lots of hoopla. The "hook"—that compelling reason for the special—was George Washington's 250th birthday, on February 22, 1982.

When Norman pitched the idea to ABC, they asked that two former presidents, one Democrat and one Republican, serve as honorary co-chairmen to ensure that the special would be viewed as bipartisan. Norman had a good relationship with President Ford's wife, Betty, and asked to meet with her husband. Soon after President Ford agreed to participate, we realized that finding a former Democratic president would be a little more difficult. At the time, Jimmy Carter was not very popular. We landed on the idea of approaching President Johnson's widow, Lady Bird, and I knew exactly who to call.

My dad first came to LBJ's attention shortly after he returned from the Korean War and started clerking at a law firm in Austin, Texas. His plan was to work for the Texas attorney general, but he got a call that set his life on a different path. Johnson was looking for a new assistant and a friend suggested Dad for the position. His mentor at the law firm nearly fell out of his chair when Dad mentioned the offer. "You have a chance to learn at the knee of the master when it comes to federal legislation and how the federal government works. There is no question that you should think long and hard about taking this remarkable opportunity." He took his mentor's advice and met with Johnson for the first time at the LBJ ranch in August 1957.

As Dad remembers it, LBJ called and said, "I've just passed the most important Civil Rights Act in eighty years, and I'm going to the ranch and wonder if you and your little lady might come out so we could spend the weekend together." They met, and over the course of two days, Johnson described all that he hoped to do while in the Senate and succeeded in inspiring Dad, who decided to accept LBJ's offer for one year. That year turned into sixteen working with Johnson both officially and unofficially until Johnson's death in 1973. Dad was more than happy to make a call on our behalf to see whether Lady Bird Johnson would consider co-chairing the proposed television special. Mrs. Johnson agreed to meet with us at the LBJ Presidential Library at the University of Texas in Austin.

Our trip to Austin had an inauspicious beginning. The night before we were to leave, Norman was in a car accident. He survived, but his mouth had smashed into the steering wheel, resulting in a monstrously swollen lip. Ever the good sport, he got on the plane with a lip that was right up there with Cyrano de Bergerac's nose. Mrs. Johnson's daughter Luci joined us for lunch and the lip was never mentioned until Norman brought it up. I wish I had been more observant of the room and other details that day, but I was focused on *why* we were there. I had confidence in Norman to make the compelling argument for Mrs. Johnson to lend her support to the TV special, but to my surprise, after she listened attentively, she graciously replied, "Oh, I don't think so. I'm a warrior no more."

Lady Bird Johnson had fought countless battles to improve the lives of millions of people before, during, and after her husband's presidency. When she said she was a warrior no more, I understood the unspoken reference to her many battle scars. She had been in the political arena all her life—and there comes a time when one gets to say, "No more." Luci, however, inferred the weight her mother's support would carry, and after we left it was Luci who convinced her mother to agree, giving us our Democratic co-chair.

Once we had the co-chairs in place and the blessing of the executives at ABC, we started an extraordinary journey of meeting with great American scholars along with some of the best talent in the business to fill out the story we wanted to tell and the people who we wanted to tell it. We met with director and choreographer Bob Fosse (*Cabaret, All That Jazz, Sweet Charity*), the screenwriter Peter Stone (*1776, Charade*), the actor/choreographer/director Tommy Tune (*Hello Dolly, The Boy Friend*), Lorne Michaels, the creator and visionary behind *Saturday Night Live*, and so many others who had agreed to come on board as consultants.

I think one of my favorite meetings was with Jim Henson, the creator of *The Muppets*. We wanted a segment in the show to appeal to the younger people in the audience and hoped that we could convince Henson to create something with Miss Piggy, Kermit, and the gang. He loved the idea and produced a very funny sketch with his beloved characters to illustrate the "true" story behind the founding of our country. Of course, like all classic Muppet sketches it ended with a funny song with Miss Piggy making a grand entrance as

Lady Liberty. Big Bird showed up to the event in person and received the loudest cheer of the night.

Then there was the question of who should host the show. We wanted a trusted American and approached Martin Sheen, who would one day play another trusted American—President Bartlet on *West Wing*. I have to confess our meeting with Sheen was way more fun than I had expected. He came to Norman's house in Brentwood to discuss the part and decided to read a scene. Since no one had been cast at that point, I read the role of the Young Girl who questions the future of America, eventually played by Kristy McNichol. When the scene ended, Martin turned to me and said, "You were good. Real good." An actress at last; his compliment made my entire week—if not month!

Norman also reached out to Bud Yorkin to co-executive produce the special with him. While Bud focused on the overall production, Norman and a small team of writers worked around the clock with a daunting mission before them—to encapsulate 250 years of American history into 90 entertaining minutes. If that wasn't enough, *I Love Liberty* was to be filmed live in front of 10,000 people at the Los Angeles Sports Arena. I worked closely on the entire development of the special and also kept an eye on the other projects we were managing at the same time. I never lost sight of *Wrinkle*.

The importance of timing for any project is one of the truisms in show business. The top films in 1980 were *The Empire Strikes Back, Any Which Way You Can, Coal Miner's Daughter,* and *Smokey and the Bandit II*—not the best timing for a fantasy about an insecure young girl who finds her place in the universe. We had to find a way to convey *Wrinkle's* broad scope and universal appeal to create the compelling argument that this was the right time for this film. The selection of the screenwriter was key. We wanted to find a screenwriter who was not only talented, but who was considered very prestigious, representing our aspirations for a major motion picture.

The entire executive team offered screenwriter suggestions, and in the summer of 1981, we landed on Sir Robert Bolt. There was no one at that time who had a more impressive track record, and hiring Bolt to write *Wrinkle* would definitely make a statement. He came to prominence as the screenwriter for David Lean's masterpiece *Lawrence of Arabia* and later won two Academy Awards for writing *Dr. Zhivago* and *A Man for All Seasons*. Everyone loved the idea, including Madeleine.

In October 1981, Norman sent Bolt a copy of the book along with a beautiful letter that conveyed how thrilled we were about the possibility of Bolt realizing *A Wrinkle in Time* as a screenplay. Norman wrote, "It's so easy to get hyperbolic in our business, but for us, despite the simple qualities of *A Wrinkle in Time*, we feel it has profound philosophic meaning for all people of all ages. At a time in the world's history when hope and faith and love are in such short supply, *Wrinkle* can make a special contribution to peoples' needs."

A month later, despite all that was happening on several fronts with *I Love Liberty*, Bolt agreed to come to New York to discuss the book. I just kept saying to myself, "*Lawrence of Arabia, Dr. Zhivago, A Man for All Seasons, A Wrinkle in Time*"— it all sounds great together. Our only concern was that Bob had had a stroke in 1979 that impaired his ability to speak. At that first meeting we found ourselves finishing his sentences, but we were confident that the impairment would not matter. The deal was finalized and Robert Bolt was hired to write the first screenplay of *A Wrinkle in Time*. We were overjoyed, convinced that he would capture all we wished for the film.

On February 22, 1982, *I Love Liberty* was filmed in front of 10,000 people at the Los Angeles Sports Arena. Norman seemed like the pied piper of patriotism because he was able to bring together such a phenomenal group of celebrities. Senator Barry Goldwater played a role in a big extravaganza of balloons, confetti, singers, dancers, bands, and even roller skaters gliding around the arena. Accompanied by the US Air Force band, Barbra Streisand sang an elegantly staged version of *America the Beautiful* that was taped in London. Jane Fonda spoke of her late father Henry Fonda's friendship with John Wayne—they disagreed on all things political but admired one another very much.

Robin Williams did a very funny impersonation of the American flag, and Christopher Reeve, Patty Duke, LeVar Burton, Judd Hirsch, Madge Sinclair, Michael Horse, Geri Jewell, Rod Steiger, Dick van Patton, and several others participated in vignettes dramatizing different turning points in American history. Between the dramatic scenes, there were familiar patriotic songs and lots of tap dancing. Norman's friendship with and admiration for the contemporary pop artist Roy Lichtenstein resulted in a fabulous piece he did of Lady Liberty holding her torch that we used in our marketing campaign.

The unabashed patriotism we all hoped to convey was present from the start of the show. It opened on a young boy's face leading a chorus in a song entitled *Liberty Calls* that had been written for the special, which then segued to Burt Lancaster as Judge Learned Hand (no relation) swearing in a new group of immigrants. It was Judge Hand's famous speech that had been delivered in 1929 that became the premise for the entire show.

> Liberty lies in the hearts of men and women and when it dies there, no constitution, no court, no law, can save it. What, then, is the spirit of liberty? I cannot define it, I can only tell you my own faith. The spirit of liberty is the spirit that is not always sure that it is right.
>
> The spirit of liberty is the spirit that seeks to understand the minds of other men and women; the spirit of liberty is the spirit that weighs their interests alongside of its own, without bias; the spirit of liberty remembers that even a sparrow does not fall to earth unheeded; the spirit of liberty is the spirit of Him who, two thousand years ago, taught mankind a lesson it has never learned, but has never quite forgotten . . . that someday there may be a kingdom where the least shall be heard side by side with the greatest. Congratulations, Americans!

It took an army of people to mount the show. I get chills recalling the moment before we went live. The sound of 10,000 voices was exhilarating—though I was also filled with fear about what could go wrong in a live taping. Then an incredible calm came over me. I thought about all that had happened to get us to this moment. The multitude of meetings across the country in creating "People For" and hundreds more in the development of *I Love Liberty*—all with people equally passionate about The American Way. We had done it. We had created an event to show young people that the individual still matters; that there is reason to believe in the future rather than despair of it—and that we must strengthen the common chords that connect us as humans and as citizens.

I thought of when Mrs. Johnson said that she was a warrior no more—but I thought every single person performing that night, everyone involved with People For the American Way, and everyone who made *I Love Liberty* possible were warriors. From the Lutheran minister Charles Bergstrom who wrote his letter to Congress, to Robin Williams who, in his incomparable way, brought the spirit of the American flag alive. In that moment, I realized how fortunate I was to work with such warriors.

I Love Liberty was a great testament to Norman's passion about the American Way and his consummate skills as a writer/producer. It has been in his DNA to entertain—to make people laugh, to have fun, and to be engaged with the world around us—and to feel gratitude and hope. Someone once said that Norman was always in a "continual lovers quarrel with America," and I thought that was the best characterization of him. In all that he did, the narrative remained the same; that we can disagree and still find common chords that bring us together in harmony.

A private screening of *I Love Liberty* was held for dozens of senators and members of Congress in Washington, DC, the week before it aired. The special received several Emmy nominations that year. Forty years later, People For the American Way continues to counter the religious right's divisive message in communities across America.

4
Working with Madeleine

To write a story, to paint a picture,
to compose a sonata or a symphony is a
religious activity, because it is an act of creation!

MADELEINE L'ENGLE

I wonder if the seeds of becoming a warrior are planted in childhood. When the Santa Ana winds blew through the window that night in the fall of 1963, Madeleine's story introduced me to the lifelong belief that a young girl could be a warrior. Up until that time, I had always looked to my dad to solve any problem. After reading *Wrinkle*, I thought I might have within me the courage to fight back any darkness. It was a vague concept that hadn't fully germinated, but the seed was definitely planted. Robert Louis Stevenson said it best, "Don't judge each day by the harvest you reap, but by the seeds you plant."

It took more than two years after we acquired the rights to *Wrinkle* before work with Madeleine began in earnest. In January 1982, Norman and his business partner, Jerry

Perenchio, purchased Embassy Pictures. Shortly afterwards, Dale Pollack, a journalist with the *LA Times*, interviewed Norman, Jerry, and Alan Horn about their new direction. They announced that *A Wrinkle in Time* would be their first project and was due to commence filming in the summer of 1983. I was so confident that the film would be made that I drove around with a license plate that read "AWIT 1983." The only troubling part about that announcement was that we had no script, no director, and no stars.

The pace of getting a film made seemed so much slower than in television. I thought that adapting the book to film would be like watching the writers meet with Norman on a Monday with a show ready to tape on a Friday—or maybe a *little* longer since a situation comedy lasted only twenty-six minutes, while a film was 90–120 minutes long. I was surprised to think it could possibly take four years from the time we optioned the book to its presumed release in 1983. The fact that a two-time Academy Award winner would start writing in the spring of 1982 gave me plenty of reason to believe this movie was going to be made. Robert Bolt would know how to adapt this book—he had done it before with previous adaptations. I knew he would do it again with *A Wrinkle in Time*. On top of that, Norman was one of the most successful writer/producers in the entertainment industry, and I didn't doubt his ability to make this movie happen now that we finally had such an acclaimed writer.

We thought that *Wrinkle* had the potential to be something very special—maybe even a classic. Jean Houston, one of the founders of the Human Potential Movement, once described

Wrinkle to me in terms of a new mythic tale. She thought that Madeleine had tapped into something very deep in the human psyche. She said, "Since *A Wrinkle in Time*'s existence, it has virtually taken on the status of a world story, of a world myth. We are becoming citizens in a universe larger than our aspirations, more complex than all our dreams. People are reaching out with love across the cosmos, embracing different forms and possibilities. We are being called upon to really redefine the human condition and children are critical to this."

Dr. Houston told me of an encounter she once had with a twelve-year-old Aboriginal in the outback of Australia. He came up to her and said, "Hey, mate, when are they going to make a movie of *A Wrinkle in Time*?" Curious, she asked him, "What does it have to do with you?"

"Oh, it's about us; it's about simple people, it's about people who [others] think are simple—and they are, but they are also profound. They know the hope of the world rides with us who hold the deep knowledge. Other people think we're just kids or we're just simple, but we're not. We hold the key." Prophetically, Jean added, "Your movie will be made when we are ready for it."

Bob Bolt's task, with our support, was to translate this mythic tale into a cinematic experience for the child in all of us—whether 10 or 100 years old. In March, Madeleine had an enjoyable phone conversation with Bolt, and by mid-April, he flew to Los Angeles to start working with us on the adaptation. The conversations between Norman and Bob were inspired—the hopeful beginnings for a truly exceptional film. The stroke Bob had in 1979 made it very difficult for him to express himself, and I found his determination to push through his difficulties very moving.

In our writers' conferences, I began to better understand the hard work ahead of us to adapt the story for film. First, decide who and what to transfer from book to screenplay. Second, establish the tone of the film. It starts off as a mystery— where is father and who are those strange women?—and evolves into a fantastical adventure. Third, to understand that some of the characters in the book have to change for the film, specifically Aunt Beast and the brain.

I was energized to be in the same room with the two of them. "What if we open on a group of international scientists in a desert somewhere who have gathered to witness Dr. Murry's tesser?" asked Bob. And Norman replied, "Yes, maybe there is a general arguing with a scientist over wasting government funds on something so far-fetched and the scientist defends the need to embrace the unknown." Norman added, "Maybe the Ladies are there." Bob asked,"What think you of Vanessa Redgrave?" I listened to them go back and forth and thought *What am I doing here?* On the one hand, I had instigated the entire thing— and on the other I felt unqualified to be in the same room with them. Bob's persistence despite his difficulty speaking inspired me to keep pushing through my own moments of self-doubt. I came to understand that listening was okay, and maybe even helpful. What I brought to the table was something neither of them had: my experience of reading *Wrinkle* as a young girl. I was the audience for this film, and was able to share with them the gist of the conversations I had had with Madeleine about the characters and themes.

As with everything Norman did, he felt the story had to resonate with the times—to determine the compelling reason why this movie ought to be made now. One of the major themes in *Wrinkle* is the courage of the individual to triumph over authoritarianism, and we could see this being played out across the country in the early 1980s. Our efforts to counter groups like the Moral Majority made us more aware of the impact the religious right's singular view in all issues was having on small communities everywhere.

Authors such as George Orwell, Arthur Miller, John Steinbeck—and even Madeleine L'Engle—were being banned in school libraries and removed from school reading lists. *A Wrinkle in Time* was banned because conservative Christians believed the depiction of the three Mrs Ws encouraged witchcraft. They also didn't like Madeleine's embrace of new scientific discoveries influencing her more inclusive view of God. This attitude towards the written word played out in Texas where even the *American Heritage Dictionary* was banned because it listed the word "bed" as a verb. In the early 1980s, teaching the theory of evolution still had to include the faith-based belief about creationism.

Another kind of conformity was starting to emerge in corporations: Publishers were eager to avoid controversy and preserve their bottom line, so they were reluctant to publish books including the theory of evolution. Less risk-taking in ideas meant less risk-taking in the bottom line. What we saw happening in the present mirrored the world our central characters inhabited in *A Wrinkle in Time* and the evil they faced on the dark planet, Camazotz. The book was still relevant even though it had been written twenty years earlier.

We wanted to help Bob in every way we could, and early on we invited Robert Blalack, a recipient of an Academy Award for his visual effects work on the original *Star Wars*, to join our conversations. We thought, and Bob agreed, that it would be helpful to have a visual effects artist assist in conceptualizing what the different planets might look like. Blalack had such innovative ideas, but the technology probably hadn't been invented yet to actualize them. Even so, it was so much fun to imagine the possibilities and ask the question, "What if?" Bob stayed in LA for a week and then flew back to London with the intention of completing his first draft in late summer.

With the purchase of Embassy Pictures, Norman's film project *Religion* moved to the front burner. As soon as Bob was on a plane, Norman and I flew to New York to meet with the two police officers to discuss their continued involvement with the Universal Life Church (ULC). We were surprised by how seriously the officers had come to take their responsibilities as ministers. They seemed to have a new purpose bigger than themselves, which was an unexpected development—for us as much as for them. They had originally been drawn to the ULC for the tax savings, which had interested us in them, but then they discovered that ministering to others was personally rewarding. We were still interested in pursuing the idea of two cops struggling to make ends meet who come upon the Universal Life Church as a means of getting rich, with one getting religion. We had high hopes for the film, and hired a new writer to work on the screenplay.

Bob's first draft of *A Wrinkle in Time* arrived in October. Sadly, despite being beautifully written, it didn't reflect much of what we had discussed in our writers' conferences. I had been so excited about the possible outcome and was deeply disappointed when it didn't work. It turned out that the contractual clause about not changing characters and themes didn't guarantee that screenwriters would capture the characters and themes as described in the book. Bolt's draft suffered from what I would witness over and over again in the decades that followed—finding a balance between a screenwriter's need to bring their interpretation to the material while staying true to the essence of the book. Bolt wrote a fairy tale that was more make-believe than a mythic tale. Mythic tales feel realistic, with characters swept up in a journey to gain wisdom and then bring that wisdom back home. I knew how real the story was to the readers I had met across the country—it wasn't just a fantasy, but a reflection of how they saw themselves.

Bob set his version in a small English village and made Meg eight years old, failing to understand that she was a young adolescent girl struggling with her self-image. He also hadn't set up Meg's faults as the very qualities that enabled her to triumph in the end. Norman and I had spent hours with him discussing how to do this as well as much more that added complexity, a sense of urgency, and humor.

On the outside, I remained upbeat as if I believed that the screenplay would improve with a second draft, but on the inside, I was worried that we were too far apart to make the collaboration work. One of the most difficult responsibilities of a producer is letting someone go, made harder when it was someone accomplished and admired. When he supervised multiple TV series, Norman was known for letting people go immediately if they weren't right for a part. If the dress rehearsal was on a Friday and the taping was on Monday, he would spend the weekend to find someone else. He made that same unequivocal call after he read Bolt's screenplay. It was gut-wrenching to read Bob's handwritten reply; this two-time Academy Award winner was genuinely taken aback that he was no longer participating in the project.

Who on earth would we get to replace him? It had taken a year to hire Bob and the thought of another year passing was depressing not to mention potentially very costly. Determined to prove that we should keep moving forward, I spent days breaking the book down scene by scene, plot point by plot point, and by the character and story arcs, and fell in love all over again with why I loved this book. It illuminated for young people all that we were trying to do with the creation of People For the American Way and with I Love Liberty—that the individual matters and there is reason to believe in the future, not to despair of it. Norman read my summary and agreed we had the rights to something very special; we just had to find the team to make it happen. I called Madeleine to inform her that Bob's script had taken the story in a different direction than the one we had desired and we were going to have to rethink our next steps.

During that conversation, we discussed the idea of Madeleine writing the screenplay. While she had never written a screenplay before, it seemed like an attractive option that would not cause us to lose momentum. If a project loses momentum, it can gradually fade away, which was the last thing I wanted to happen. Madeleine had only one conversation with Bolt, which is normal when a screenwriter is hired to adapt an author's work. He wanted the freedom to approach the material in his own way without the author present. We thought that maybe we needed more direct input from Madeleine. She agreed that Bob's script went in an unexpected direction and sent us notes on how she would proceed. Her feedback was accompanied with a brief letter that expressed her enthusiasm for the opportunity to write the screenplay, "It's always good to talk to you—and especially today, which showed me that we can work together—I know we can! Herewith some hot-off-the typewriter unrevised responses to RB's screenplay. They are not in cement, but I think they give you an idea of what I can do."

Madeleine's notes clearly conveyed the Meg in the book and Norman was willing to give the collaboration a try. He also took the time to dictate his thoughts on how to adapt the book resulting in a twelve-page, single-spaced partial treatment fleshing out the Murry family and the Mrs Ws (the three celestial beings) filled with humor and very relatable characters. He came up with a scene of the Murry family playing charades at the space center waiting for their dad to depart. He had invented the idea that the audience would see Dr. Murry with his family before he disappears, to visually establish the strong bond the family had with him. Meg was playful and engaged with the game, bossing everyone around. If my scene breakdown restored Norman's faith in the project, his partial treatment completely affirmed my hopes and dreams. This movie could work!

As soon as we closed our deal with Madeleine to write the screenplay, I was on a plane to New York to spend time with her. My mission was to serve as a sounding board as she thought through ideas for the screenplay. I had spent the past two years discussing the book with Norman and had sat in on every discussion with Robert Bolt, so I felt comfortable doing the same with her, but I had never done this completely on my own. I had always assumed Norman would lead the development of the script—but now I was flying solo, literally. I didn't let on, but I felt anxious about what was expected of me—what if I failed to help her in the way she needed?

I thought about the advice my mother gave me in high school when feeling unsure of myself in a situation—just smile. I must have been voted Most Likely to Succeed in high school not because I knew something others didn't, but because when I didn't know what to do, I smiled and was willing to dive into the unknown. Sometimes I sank like a log, but more often than not I learned how to swim. This was my strategy with Madeleine. I didn't know exactly what I was supposed to do, but I was going to try to figure it out and hope for the best. I relied on Madeleine to lead the way and felt confident that I was a good sounding board.

I met Madeleine and her husband, Hugh, at their apartment on the Upper West Side of New York City, and we drove from there to their home in Goshen, Connecticut. That drive was unforgettable; I had to ride in the back seat sitting next to their Irish setter, and the dog's smell was overwhelming. I love dogs, and would come to love this dog, but I kept the window open the entire drive for a whiff of fresh air. I was so excited to be with Madeleine and Hugh, I never let on that I was feeling sick the whole drive. It was worth it though; the moment we pulled into the driveway, I could see that the Murrys' 200-year-old white clapboard house, described in *Wrinkle*, was modeled after their home, Crosswicks.

The first thing Hugh did when we walked through the back door into the kitchen was to offer to make me a liverwurst and cream cheese sandwich—the same sandwich Charles Wallace offers his mother on that fateful dark and stormy night. I could tell that Hugh was very pleased with his little inside joke. Seeing the twinkle in his eye, I knew this would be one of the most special times in my life. I let go of my fear of failing and felt the joy of standing in the kitchen that looked so much like the kitchen described in the book. It was as if I had been transported into the Murry home.

The house had been rundown when they bought it in 1952, but Madeleine explained that with lots of love and rolls of wallpaper it had become their family home. Madeleine took me on a tour of the house, and as we walked up the stairs to the attic, I swear I heard a creak on one of the steps. Once at the top of the stairs, I peered into the main area and saw the ping-pong table that Meg bumped into and her dollhouse sitting off in a corner. The high point was walking into Meg's bedroom and looking out the window where she saw the frenzied wind lashing through the trees. It was almost surreal to sit on the bed and look out that window. Madeleine always conveyed an infectious sense of joy and wonder, and I felt that same kind of joy and wonder being with her in that moment.

She had transformed an old chicken coop above the garage into her writing space; her family always referred to the room as The Tower. She wrote *A Wrinkle in Time* there, and it was where we worked on her screenplay. It quickly became clear to me why the clause that prohibited changing characters and themes was so important to her; she didn't want to change *anything*. Usually, when someone or a company options film rights, they want the freedom to make any changes they see fit with no restrictions—which was Madeleine's greatest fear about signing any agreement. There were moments when I thought the only thing that would satisfy her was to put the words from the book onto the screen and have the audience

The Tower, Madeleine L'Engle's office at Crosswicks where she wrote *A Wrinkle in Time* and where we worked on the screenplay

follow along with a bouncing ball. My goal was to somehow get her to let go of her fears.

We had talked about the characters and themes over the years, but now we had a new focus and purpose—we needed to use whatever ideas had inspired the creation of the book to aid us in the creation of the film. As a way for Madeleine to re-imagine the book as a film, I thought it might help to revisit whatever was occurring in her life when she wrote the book. What had influenced her? Who inspired the Mrs Ws? Where did the idea of the tesseract arise? Why the religious references? I thought maybe if we cast a look backwards it would help Madeleine move forward.

To understand *A Wrinkle in Time* is to understand it is a kaleidoscope of her own personal story. She was born in 1918 and spent her early childhood years in New York City. Her father was a foreign correspondent during World War I, her mother a pianist, and Madeleine was their only child. Both parents loved to entertain and were away from the apartment often. Madeleine was left in the care of Mrs. O (O'Connell) who served as the inspiration for the character Aunt Beast. No matter what mischief Madeleine caused, Mrs. O loved her.

At an early age, Madeleine loved to read, and from her youthful point of view, she equated the stories she read in the Bible to those in the great storybooks by Hans Christian Andersen, the Brothers Grimm, and Lewis Carroll, among others. As she said, they were "all marvelous stories about unqualified people. You know God never chose anyone qualified to do anything? The point was that if you were qualified, you could do it yourself—you didn't need anyone. If you're not qualified, you know you need help." She went on to explain that in all archetypal stories it's the unqualified character that ends up alone in the forest and has to rely on the kindness of strangers. Meg Murry was *unqualified* at the start of her journey and had to listen to Mrs Whatsit, Mrs Who, and Mrs Which to find her way home.

I was a little unnerved at first by Madeleine's word usage and literary references to classic poems and books that she assumed I had read. Once she started to quote an English poet from the seventeenth century by the name of Thomas Traherne. Without skipping a beat she said, "Know him?" She then continued without waiting for my answer, "He starts out with 'Surely Adam and Eve in Paradise had no more sweet and glorious apprehension than I' and then he lists all the pleasures of the senses. 'But without further ado I was corrupted by the dirty devices of this world. Now I must unlearn and become as it were a little child again so that I may enter the kingdom of heaven.'" She continued, "So, in a sense, writing *A Wrinkle in Time* was an act of unlearning—to go back to that willingness to look at new ideas, to not be afraid of looking at new things. And, the new math I was reading was exciting. It asked questions and it didn't insist on rigid answers!"

I didn't know what she meant by "unlearn." I was trying to learn everything, especially when I felt so unqualified being in the same conversation with her. I didn't read seventeenth century poets for inspiration but was in awe that she found beauty and insight in them. It was clear where Mrs Who's quotes came from—it was as natural as breathing for Madeleine to quote from a variety of sources in almost every conversation I ever had with her. As I sat there listening to her, I wondered how I was going to keep up, and how we could use what she was saying in the film adaptation. How could we use her intellectual ideas and translate them into a cinematic experience for young people?

When Madeleine was about eleven years old, her family moved to Europe for her father's health. She said his lungs had been damaged by mustard gas during World War I—but the truth is he may have needed a change of scenery for his alcoholism. I came to find out that Madeleine was like that. She would tell a story about her life so convincingly and then I would later learn that story was only partially true. I became good at listening with a discerning ear. What was undoubtedly true is that she had been traumatized at an early age when, without warning, her parents dropped her off at a Swiss boarding school. They took a drive and she had no idea of the destination; they arrived at the school, her parents introduced her to the headmaster, and they left. At the age of twelve she felt lonely and abandoned which would give her this amazing ability to accurately capture the yearnings of a lonely and insecure girl. When her parents returned to the States a few years later, Madeleine was sent to high school at Ashley Hall, a boarding school in South Carolina. She loved it. There, Madeleine found the acceptance and recognition she craved.

Madeleine attended Smith College in Massachusetts, and after graduation, she headed to New York City with a girlfriend for a career in the theater. She had developed a love for the theater and wrote plays while in high school, and hoped to make a career of it. In NYC, she became an assistant to Eva

Le Gallienne who was an accomplished actress, producer, and manager. She was an influential force in creating the idea of off-Broadway, producing shows in smaller theaters not yet ready for the bigger theaters on Broadway. Madeleine greatly admired Le Gallienne who was the inspiration for Mrs Which, the wisest of the three Mrs Ws.

While on tour with Le Gallienne's production of *The Cherry Orchard*, Madeleine met and fell in love with Hugh. He was an actor who would later become known for playing Dr. Charles Tyler on the TV soap opera *All My Children*. He was clearly the inspiration for the character Calvin in *Wrinkle*. If Madeleine was like a supernova, it was Hugh who kept her feet on the ground and patiently edited her work. He had beautiful blue eyes and a gentle soul. Even though she hated smoking, Hugh let me stand by the early morning fire he built each day while I was at Crosswicks so I could sneak in a cigarette. (My session with the hypnotist during that first month on the job working for Norman didn't take.)

When Madeleine and Hugh left New York City to live full time in Goshen in 1952, the population was fewer than a 1,000 people, and it's only 2,000 today. Hugh ran the one general store, and when Madeleine wasn't helping him at the store, she was caring for two small children, active in the community, and writing at night. When I asked her how she managed it all, she replied, "I wasn't a very good housekeeper!" They had moved to the country to get away from the frightening rise of McCarthyism. Joseph McCarthy, a senator from Wisconsin, was determined to wipe out Communism in every nook and cranny of American society, no matter how many lives he destroyed in the process.

Of that time, Madeleine wrote in her journal:

> The McCarthy hearings are so incredible that it is
> almost impossible to believe they are happening in this
> country. If McCarthy comes out on top it is going to be
> a ghastly tragedy for this country. The ghosts of Hitler
> and Stalin are leering over our shoulders and their
> icy breaths are unutterably terrifying. If we succumb
> to fascism there will be no democracy left in the
> world and civilization as we know it, civilization that
> produced Shakespeare and Raleigh, Bach and Da Vinci,
> Beethoven and Moliere, Pasteur and Pascal, Einstein
> and Freud, Shaw and Racine, Mill and Schopenhauer,
> Brahms and Milton, will have vanished as completely
> as though indeed we had loosed the H-bomb in all
> its horror.

Many of these names later appeared in *Wrinkle* when Meg, Charles Wallace, and Calvin learn about the fighters on Earth.

During our work together, I mentioned the difficulty we had in earlier conversations with Bolt about the connection between the darkness spreading throughout the galaxies, the It, and the Man with the Red Eyes. Listening, she grew irritated and exclaimed "Evil exists!" It wasn't the definition of evil that mattered to her, but the fact that it exists, and will always exist, in many forms. She said that the goal was not to conquer the Darkness, but to conquer our *fear* of the Darkness—and by doing so, weaken its power over us. That was the biggest problem every writer would face in tackling the screenplay—including Madeleine. How to take that abstract idea and make it work in a film.

When growing up, Madeleine had been terrified of war. "I remember my feeling of utter horror when Mussolini and his men marched into Ethiopia. I thought here it is—here is another war. I have lived in a century of nothing but war, and war is the Dark. I spent the rest of my life lighting candles [to avoid giving] into the Darkness." She explained that she thought there was a kind of macro darkness, like war, and a kind of micro darkness that we can carry within ourselves, like feeling lost, insecure, and or hating oneself. She wanted the audience to understand those things about Meg's journey. In overcoming her fear of the darkness on Camazotz to rescue Charles Wallace, Meg overcomes her personal fears; one impacts the other.

When *Wrinkle* was first published, Madeleine was asked if the "It" stands for intellectual truth, which she acknowledged could be a possibility. She said, "When we limit ourselves to our controllable, little dictator minds alone we've lost a lot of ourselves. So, what I was saying, even though I didn't know it, was when we are intellect alone—and not informed by the heart or by intuition—it becomes vicious and evil." She added, "You know so many men and women ... stop growing, stop asking questions, they become afraid to ask questions. People would [ask] me, is Camazotz Russia? [But] you don't have to go to Russia, just fly out of any great American city and you fly over [Camazotz]. I wrote

Wrinkle to free youth from the restrictive fears that frighten an unimaginative adult world."

The more time I spent with Madeleine, the more I saw there were many layers to the story, and that each layer needed to be peeled back and understood in light of how it related to the whole so we could reconceptualize it as a film. I had to better understand physics, the meaning of Christianity from Madeleine's point of view, her ideas about time, the significance each character brought to the story, and her belief in the importance of free will in order to accurately capture Meg's personal quest. I wanted to help Madeleine figure out how to bring the elements that gave the book such enduring power to an equally successful movie. It all seemed slightly overwhelming at the time, but it was truly an exceptional education.

When Madeleine had been writing *Wrinkle*, she was reading about Einstein, works by German theologians, and a book about the Russian author Dostoevsky whose passion was free will, which she found very inspiring. She said, "God created us with free will so that we do have a say in our own story. It's not taken away from us, we are not manipulated, and it's not pre-ordained. If I have to say what I believe about God, it is that we are called to be co-creators. God didn't make a universe and finish it!" Madeleine believed that great things had been accomplished throughout history by inadequate and unqualified people who, because they believed they could do it, did the impossible. "I believe we can do the impossible, and that's one of the things we have to show in the film. It isn't just that we blow ourselves up, or we become like the people on Camazotz. We do have free will and we may make other choices." In *Wrinkle*, Meg makes a different choice than the inhabitants on Camazotz.

In the late 1950s, Madeleine was going through a crisis of faith and her minister recommended she read several books by German theologians, which didn't help at all. She explained, "They were telling me all about God and I didn't like what they were telling me. I think the only way one can be what one would call a 'believer' is to be a Christian Agnostic, which means, 'I love that which I cannot know.' I cannot know the power that created the galaxies. It's infinite. I am finite. I was rebelling against all these books that were giving all the answers. We don't have all the answers. All we have are the questions. All we have are stories. There is no way the finite creature can appreciate the infinite at all. To write a story, to paint a picture, to compose a sonata or a symphony is a religious activity, because it is an act of creation!"

The book has Christian undertones, but not conventional ones, which is why conservative Christians wanted to have it banned. Over time, I came to understand that Madeleine's view of Christianity was part of a centuries-long tradition of adapting our understanding of the Bible to our human understanding of the evolving world around us. After Darwin's theory of evolution became known, there was a big leap to see the Bible as story. Madeleine herself took another big leap after reading Einstein's discovery of the theory of relativity. The questions she asked herself about the meaning of Christianity in relation to new scientific discoveries were powerful:

We now know that the world is made up of tiny, tiny
particles and if you separate them everything falls apart.
We exist because they come together. If they didn't
come together, we wouldn't exist—that's a kind of scary
thought. I like the fact that I exist and I wouldn't like not
to exist. We have to find out who we are in relation to the
world we live in—and the world we live in is based on
particle physics. We have to learn about particle physics
in order to ask the question who am I? Where am I?
What's my place in the universe?

I didn't have Madeleine's knowledge of physics, but I did
love thinking about the vastness of the galaxies. As a child, I
had been fascinated by John Glenn's 1962 flight orbiting the
earth, and I had the good fortune to be at the Johnson Space
Center when Neil Armstrong walked on the moon in 1969, but
I knew nothing about a tesseract or hypercube. Topics like
multiple dimensions and unified field theory may be more
accessible today, but they were not in 1959. Madeleine used
Einstein's theories to create three marvelous otherworldly
creatures, Mrs Which, Mrs Who, and Mrs Whatsit, who
transformed from matter to energy and were able to move
effortlessly through time and space.

When we first started working together, she suggested I
read *Einstein's Universe* by Nigel Calder. She said, "It's an
easy read," and I laughed—no book about Einstein's theories
would be easy for me to read. Nonetheless, it was exciting
to discover Einstein from her point of view. Reading about
Einstein's theories must have done for Madeleine what

reading *A Wrinkle in Time* did for me—it was Einstein who provided a portal into the extraordinary, mysterious universe that set her curiosity on fire. He once said, "I want to know how God created this world. I am not interested in this or that phenomenon. I want to know His thoughts; the rest are details." I think Madeleine did too.

She once wrote that *A Wrinkle in Time* has meant different things to different people at different times in their lives, and that was certainly true for her. Her explanations of the characters and themes evolved, and her perspective grew in the passing years—as she did. She was Meg. She once said of her main character in *Wrinkle*: "There are a lot of Megs in this country. I think what draws people to her is that they recognize themselves in her. They feel unattractive. They don't realize they are attractive. They feel stupid. They know they are bright, but they don't understand it. Love and respect for herself was what Meg needed. She didn't know how good she was or how beautiful she was and how sensitive and real and lovely she was." There was something else about her young heroine that Madeleine believed—she was capable of doing more than she knew on behalf of those she loved. In the climax, this is exactly what Meg does; she is able to find the courage she didn't know she had to save her brother.

In the summer of 1959, Madeleine and Hugh took their kids on a camping trip. Somewhere near the Painted Desert, the names of the celestial trio—Mrs Whatsit, Mrs Who, and Mrs Which—came to her. They were, as she said, "a free gift." She turned around in the car and said, "Hey, kids, what do you think of these three names? I'll have to put them in my book."

When the children were asleep, she and Hugh sat by the dying embers of the campfire over which she had cooked dinner and stared up at the stars. She knew all the stars are suns, and that many of those suns have planets, and that certainly Earth is not the only inhabited planet. When the family returned home she said, "All of these things began working together in a slow cooker, Hugh went off to do a play, and my mother asked what are you going to do while Hugh is gone? [I replied] well, I'll write a book, of course, and I sat down and typed out, "It was a dark and stormy night . . ."

From the first time Madeleine and I met at the restaurant high atop the World Trade Center to the last time I saw her shortly before she died in 2007, we carried on a twenty-five-year long conversation about *A Wrinkle in Time*. I wish I had the words to explain our relationship, but it was as if we both connected to our adolescent selves when we were together discussing the themes and characters in the book. The trust between us was total. Of all the conversations we had, the most moving was when she spoke of the rejections she endured trying to get *Wrinkle* published. As she paced about the small room acting out what it felt like to receive twenty-six rejections, her voice became intense, angry, and vulnerable all at once. I saw a woman who felt hurt and frustrated about the dismissal of her work.

"Twenty-six times I heard the word *no*. I wanted to give up and thought I'd never write again. Then I realized I *had* to write and I took the cover off the typewriter and started a new book." As I watched her, it hit me hard that this woman who had known such success also knew such self-doubt and despair.

It was clear that the book meant so much to her, because Meg's journey represented Madeleine's personal search for meaning. I swore to myself in that moment that if she could endure that kind of rejection to get the book published, I could do the same to get the movie made. No one knew better than she how difficult it was going to be. It never occurred to me in the early days of working with Madeleine that my quest to adapt the book for film would become my own search for meaning.

On my last night at Crosswicks, we were sitting by one of Hugh's roaring fires and she said, "Promise me that you will use the one line in the book that means the most to me." "Of course," I replied, not having a clue which line meant the most to her. She said, "'Like and equal are not the same thing at all.' Do you understand what that means?" I said something lame like, "I think I do," knowing that I hadn't given it a thought until she said this, and feeling surprised that this line was so important to her.

She said that all his life the character Calvin had to live under camouflage until he met Meg. It was an act for him to pretend that he was not as bright as he really was—he took on a persona as a track star and basketball player, but he had to put his mind under a bushel until he discovered Meg and the rest of the Murry family. She elaborated, "He goes on this journey and learns to be himself . . . and to be who he is. It's what both Meg and Calvin learn during their adventure. We all want to become and be seen for who we fully are. I suppose it's the hardest thing any of us have to learn. He was trying to be *like* something he wasn't, and wanted to be treated *equally* for who he really was as a person."

Her description about Calvin living his life hidden under a bushel gave me pause. In some ways, I identified with Calvin as much as I did with Meg. I had always worked to be friendly and popular at all the different schools I attended in order to be accepted. Had I been living my life hidden under a bushel? Had I been trying to be something I wasn't? In that one conversation, Madeleine pushed me to think about what happened to Meg on Camazotz in a deeper way than I ever had.

In *Wrinkle*, everyone on Camazotz is alike, and if there is any aberration they are reprocessed. Meg wanted to be like everyone else to fit in at school, but once she discovers a planet where everyone is *forced* to be alike, she realizes that she had confused personality traits with value as a person—warts and all. It's a seed that Aunt Beast planted before Meg's final return to Camazotz, saying, "Things which are seen are temporal. But things which are not seen are eternal." Meg finally understands what Aunt Beast meant after Charles Wallace has been taken over by the evil force on Camazotz. She has to see Charles Wallace for who he is—not how he appears—in order to love the true Charles Wallace.

My conversation with Madeleine about "like and equal" would become the catalyst for my own self-transformation. Watching the interactions between Madeleine and Hugh at Crosswicks, enjoying long walks with her across the field behind their home, and helping cook dinner, I became aware that I had no work/life balance in my life. I hadn't taken the time to develop great personal friendships and other interests. A colleague of mine enjoyed reading recipes at night and I thought, *Recipes?!* Why did I not understand reading recipes was a worthwhile thing to do? Everything I did outside of the office—reading a book or a magazine, seeing a movie, going to a play, meeting someone for a drink or a meal—all revolved around my job. The conversations I had with Madeleine during my stay with her ignited in me the question I had never taken the time to ask—maybe because I didn't want to know the answer: Why was everything I did about work?

When my trip to Crosswicks came to an end, I felt somewhat confident that I had been a helpful sounding board and that Madeleine was more aware of how she had to collapse scenes and events to create a more visual interpretation of the story. Her first draft arrived a few months later and it was promising. When we invited her to Los Angeles, she asked that we find her a bungalow so she could work from there. I didn't understand her request; and when I repeated it to Norman he paused for a moment and laughed. He said, "Oh, she is expecting a work arrangement like they used to have in the 1940s. Things have changed. Find her a nice room at the Century Plaza Hotel." I called her back and relayed what the accommodations would be and she agreed, adding, "Ok, but make sure I have a large tub. I'm tall."

She arrived ready to work, and it was glorious to be in the same room with both Norman and Madeleine discussing *A Wrinkle in Time.* They went off on so many tangents as they started to get to know one another. Norman was her mental equal. They didn't just talk about Meg, Charles Wallace, and Calvin's backstories; they discussed the vastness of the universe and the devastating consequences of book banning. Madeleine opened up to Norman about her life before she wrote *Wrinkle*; this time I heard her story from a more personal point of view rather than the one connected to German theologians and Dostoevsky.

Living in a small New England village in the 1950s was difficult for her. No one she knew had books, or liked books, and they certainly didn't write them. Her self-confidence had suffered with the series of rejections slips she had received for other books she had written before she wrote *Wrinkle*. "I was in my thirties—a total Meg." The sermons she heard at the local Congregational Church sounded rigid and narrow. "There was no joy in what they were saying or anything that made life more abundant," she said. It was when she stumbled upon new post-Newtonian science that she found her theology. Madeleine won Norman over completely when she said, "I wrote *Wrinkle* as my affirmation of a universe in which I could believe in the power of love. I wrote it as a way to say 'yes' to life."

As soon as Norman really got who she was and where she was coming from, he was even more committed to the project. They spoke the same language and were cut from the same cloth. The conversations between those two were thought-provoking— and often very funny. They spent a week brainstorming all sorts of ideas for the film, and Madeleine loved that Norman wanted to play up the humor in the book. As Mrs Which says, "The only way to cope with something deadly serious is to treat it lightly." One of the funniest bits Norman created was a wallet that Mrs Whatsit would carry. When it was time for her to transform

Madeleine and me

into a different creature she'd take out the wallet, open it up, and watch as hundreds of plastic cardholders fell to the ground. She would scroll through them and say to herself, "No, not that one," and, "No, he's too tall," she laughs at another, then looks sheepishly at another, and so on until she triumphantly reaches the character she becomes on Uriel.

I had an epiphany of sorts when I recently reread the transcripts from our sessions together. People have often said that they didn't see what I did in *A Wrinkle in Time*, and I now realize that's because they hadn't been in the writers' meetings with Norman and Madeleine. It wasn't just the book that I wanted to adapt, but what I saw that the movie could be based on those conversations. I wanted to see the movie we envisioned together, believing it would always be something worth fighting for. It was inspiring to hear Madeleine speak about *Wrinkle* as her affirmation of a universe—her "yes" to life—coupled with Norman's genius at poking fun at the human condition, even in the fifth dimension. There is nothing more suited for poignancy and humor than a young girl who feels like an oddball and three wise women—messengers from God—trying to get her to see herself from a different dimension. The joy and excitement these two giants in their respective fields had for this movie was imprinted on my heart and soul forever.

There was something else, too, that I wasn't conscious of at the time: They both had made the impossible possible in their own lives and encouraged others to do the same. When Madeleine wrote *A Wrinkle in Time*, she was a struggling mom of three and writing when she could. She wrote a story that gave her life meaning and did it because she believed that she could—and her work influenced millions of readers. In the 1950s, Norman and his first writing partner, Ed Simmons, went door-to-door selling home furnishings while waiting to get their first break writing comedy sketches. They finally convinced Danny Thomas to give them a chance and later wrote for

Jerry Lewis and Tennessee Ernie Ford. I doubt anyone could imagine in those days that Norman would one day change the face of television and be the recipient of every major award in television, including the Kennedy Center Honor.

The time I spent with Madeleine and Norman discussing *A Wrinkle in Time* had a huge impact on me. They inspired me to dream, to believe that as impossible as it might seem, it was possible for a great movie to be made.

5
A Man's World

I'm a success today because I had
a friend who believed in me and I didn't
have the heart to let him down.

ABRAHAM LINCOLN

W hen I was a young girl, I said my prayers every night asking God to show me how to do well with my life. I hoped that included mastering the rings on the playground at Bellagio Road Elementary School in West Los Angeles. Most mornings I'd look up and see a clear blue sky while I swayed back and forth with increasing vigor, determined to win the ring competition before school started. It was on that playground where I first heard the words, "It's a man's world," and concluded that I would have to think more like a boy to do well with my life and to master the rings.

My mother, Ann Hand, didn't seem to mind that it was a man's world. She was raised in an age where that was understood and accepted. My brothers, sisters, and I didn't make it easy for her to raise young ladies and young gentlemen, but she was determined to do so. I probably heard, "Young ladies don't chew gum" a gazillion times and each time wondered why. Mom was—is—beautiful inside and out. Even when we disagreed over clothes, politics, or life in general, she loved me unconditionally.

She was raised in Houston, Texas, when Texas was a mix of the old South and the old West. The notion of Southern hospitality was in her DNA, which is why she probably thought any solution to a sticky problem was to "just smile." Her father, my Grandfather Donoghue, was a lawyer who had the gentle soul of a poet. He was tenth generation Irish and told me when I was five that we were descendants of the king of Ireland. I believed his story for years until I discovered that hundreds of years ago you could call yourself a king if you owned a castle. His uncle was one of the co-founders of Texaco Oil Company, and my mother loved to visit her great-uncle's home—at the time it was called a mansion. Her mother's side of the family could be traced back to the Huguenots who landed in Virginia in 1704 to escape religious persecution in France.

My mother's sense of patriotism and love of country was born sitting next to her parents listening to the announcer on the radio reporting on the bombing over Pearl Harbor on December 7, 1941. At the age of fifteen, she was asked to sing at the opening of the grand and luxurious Shamrock Hotel, which was the biggest social event in Houston at the time. She still lights up when she describes wearing a ball gown covered in fresh white camellias. She had every intention of studying music at the University of Texas, but she met my father at a freshman dance, and it was love at first sight.

My parents as college sweethearts, 1951

He was the student body president and unbeknownst to him she had just been voted the most beautiful freshman co-ed. Her parents weren't too keen for them to get married before she graduated, so they eloped. I loved learning that she had to crawl out the window of her rooming house, Newman Hall, to keep their plan a secret.

If you ask my dad what has been their secret to a happy marriage for over 70 years, he will quickly say, "Because we still want to be together." Their life has been filled with incredible adventures as diverse as an audience with the pope, meeting the Dalai Lama, and dinners with presidents and prime ministers around the world. When she was fifty-four, Mom started her own jewelry design firm in Washington, DC. Her American Collection has been worn by some of the most powerful and influential women and men in the nation. It was my mother's joy and love of life that instilled in me the desire to know how to make the impossible possible and—as she would insist—as long as I was a lady while doing it.

She was not a big proponent of the woman's movement when it first emerged, and neither was I. It wasn't a matter of being for or against; it was just that the three major issues facing my generation throughout high school and into college were the Vietnam War, the draft, and Watergate. I hadn't tried to get a credit card and been told I needed a man to co-sign. I didn't know a woman could be fired from the workplace if she were pregnant. I had never read Betty Friedan's groundbreaking book, *The Feminine Mystique*, nor had I heard of what she called "the problem with no name."

In the movies, I saw women who seemed happy to return to their former lives as wives and mothers after World War II. That was not what Friedan found when interviewing women who *were* wives and mothers in the 1950s. It was while working at Tandem Productions that I became aware of the importance of the Equal Rights Amendment (ERA) and learned that women only earned sixty-nine cents to every dollar a man made for the same work. It was also at Tandem where I first heard the term "consciousness-raising" as in consciousness-raising dinners to discuss a woman's role in society, and consciousness-raising topics often found in Norman's TV series.

My consciousness was profoundly raised when working with Madeleine. She really was like the women I admired in the films from the 1940s: strong, independent, and had a career despite the constraints that held most women back. When Madeleine spoke of the unqualified making the impossible possible, I heard that as it pertained to women, because most men saw women as "unqualified" for the job—not up to the task. She turned that notion on its head when she created a seemingly impossible task for a young girl to not only rescue her father and brother, but to bring back knowledge on how to fight back the darkness on Earth. The fact that a young girl got that opportunity was the real power of the story, and why I was determined to get the film made. It had the potential to raise consciousness in enduring and profound ways.

Wrinkle wasn't the only film project we were developing with strong female protagonists. In 1981, Jonathan Demme (*The Silence of the Lambs, Philadelphia, Beloved*) was just a few years into his directing career when he pitched a movie idea about Sonia Johnson who was excommunicated in 1979 from the Mormon Church for publicly supporting the ERA. Jonathan was passionate about telling this story of a wife and mother of four who found the courage to speak out in support of the Equal Rights Amendment even though it meant her church would reject her.

Claire Townsend, then a young vice president at 20th Century Fox, heard about the project and wanted to meet to discuss a possible co-venture between Embassy Pictures and Fox. She, too, was looking for possible film projects to empower women. I really admired Claire from the moment we met in her office on the Fox lot. She was a born warrior. Upon high school graduation, she, along with several of her classmates, worked with Ralph Nader investigating elder abuse in nursing homes. Their research led to Nader's book *Old Age: The Last Segregation*. Soon after she graduated from Princeton, she made her way to Los Angeles for a career in the entertainment business. Claire, along with Lucy Fisher at Warner Bros, Thom Mount and Sean Daniel at Universal, and a few others, were part of a new generation of studio executives focused on finding good stories for our generation. Unfortunately, like so many projects, the Sonia Johnson story never made it to the screen; however, Claire and I became lifelong friends. It took about five minutes for us to discover our shared love of *A Wrinkle in Time*.

Claire was the first to say to me what many of us were finding: We were the first generation of single women who had financial independence like never before. During a meeting with a group of male executives at Fox, she realized they were working to provide for their families while she was working to provide for herself. For the first time in our lives, we had what was called disposable income—money left over after paying our bills. This financial freedom made it possible to start seeking other ways for our voices to be heard. New organizations like EMILY's List encouraged women to write checks backing candidates and issues that impacted them. Up until that time, it was largely men who had written checks in support of policies and politicians.

While the fight for equal rights in the 1970s brought significant cultural change, it was still a struggle for a woman
to get in the room where decisions were made. Imagine a
male studio executive saying today to a female colleague
that she can't attend a meeting because of the swearing that
might occur; that happened to a friend of mine who was a
top studio executive. This type of comment wasn't sexual
harassment as we know it today, but it was an understated
and understood form of discrimination towards women. I
was asked so many times in meetings when I was the only
woman in the room, "What do you think is the woman's
point of view?" As if there were only one! The question was
absurd—if there had been five men in the room, there were
five different points of view.

In the early 1980s, no one knew what equality for women
in the entertainment industry ought to look like because men
had always defined power. I struggled to be heard in a room
full of men trying to get them to care about a story told from a
young girl's perspective. I wanted to be the kind of person Mr.
Perenchio had described, prepared to take a nuclear bullet to
get something done and willing to endure lots of rejection
to develop those pants made of steel, but it wasn't easy. In 1981,
everything between men and women was in flux: language,
terminology, and our behavior towards one another. One day,
a male executive at Embassy came into my office and said,
"What is this word *relationship*? I thought you just dated—or
didn't date—but this girl I'm dating wants to know if we are in
a *relationship*." It seemed especially difficult to navigate these
issues in the entertainment business because there was a long

history of exploiting women as sex objects. How to square that with this new thinking?

Tom Hanks' line, "There's no crying in baseball," in the film *A League of Their Own* about all-girls baseball teams was funny because it perfectly captured how uncomfortable the expression of emotions made most men. We weren't supposed to cry in the workplace, but women did, hidden from view in stairwells, restrooms, and closets. There were unspoken rules about how to behave in business; revealing one's feelings was not acceptable. Women who raised their voices or cried risked being labeled as difficult. The jokes about our shoulder pads

As executive assistant "dressed for success"

and the suits worn in the early '80s were spot on—they represented ways in which women could look like men, as if looking like them would make us equal.

I had several of those suits and wondered if there would ever come a time when women could show their vulnerabilities and still be taken seriously. Sitting in a screening room while waiting for others to join, I had a conversation with Norman about this very issue. I asked him when do women get to have a sense of humor? When do we get to crack jokes? Why did we have to act, talk, and look like a man to appear capable of any real authority? He didn't know what I was talking about. Then, the others walked in and I was glad I was wearing my pinstripe suit—the suit of armor for any female executive working in the entertainment business.

In addition to dressing like a man to be seen as less feminine, there was the ever-present fear of being replaced. No matter how much Norman may have appreciated my talents and contributions, there was always an underlying fear that could change. At its core, the entertainment business is mercurial, always dependent on the moods of the executives in charge, the audience, and the times in which we live. I never knew if someone would come along that better represented Norman's new interest that month. Today, if a woman is let go from one job, it isn't that difficult for her to find another, but in the industry back then, opportunities were far fewer. It is ironic that people who question why it took 40 years for something like the #MeToo movement to emerge are the same people who cower at publicly disagreeing with former President Trump for fear of being replaced. Only when women achieved financial and creative success at scale was it possible to speak truth to power.

All the successes today enjoyed by women in the entertainment business and elsewhere were hard earned, one woman at a time. I wasn't an ardent feminist, perhaps because in my late twenties I hadn't yet experienced the type of disappointment and frustration so many women did. My father used to say something he learned from Lyndon Johnson, "A half a loaf is better than no loaf, and those that complain about a half a loaf don't know what it is to go hungry." I was truly grateful to have a half a loaf. Most women of my generation had been conditioned to feel the same. I thought all I had to do was to keep my head down, work hard, and everything would turn out okay.

Unfortunately, that didn't apply to adapting *A Wrinkle in Time* for the screen. Madeleine's script ultimately failed to meet all our expectations, including her own. With all the great back and forth, ideas for character development, changes that needed to be made to the plot, and wonderful dialogue suggestions, her screenplay read like a novel and not a movie. Both Madeleine and I remained steadfast in our commitment to get it right, but Norman was being pulled into a number of new directions with the purchase of Embassy Pictures. This meant he had less and less time to devote to any one project.

In the spring of 1982, six years after I had been so thrilled to be a receptionist in Norman's office, something began changing within me too. I don't know when it started, but I think it was when Norman and I walked into the reception area of Jim Henson's office to discuss his participation in *I Love Liberty*. There is something called the "hundredth monkey effect," a hypothetical phenomenon in which a new idea takes hold the moment it reaches a critical mass—the hundredth monkey—and then spreads rapidly. I had easily attended over a hundred meetings with Norman in LA, on the road, and in New York, and I always stood by his side when he walked into an office and announced he was there for a meeting. It never occurred to me that he would include my name except for that figurative one hundredth meeting when we met with Jim Henson. I thought, *Why didn't he say my name too?* Of course, Norman was the person they wanted to meet, but in that moment, I was aware of how invisible I was.

The conversations I had with Madeleine and others were gradually changing how I saw myself and my place in the world. I had been working closely with Norman as his sounding board and helped to execute his political activities, the development of his film and television projects, and the production of *I Love Liberty*, not to mention *Wrinkle*. There was no question I was learning more than I could possibly know from him and was proud of the work we had done together—but even the invisible glue has a name. The other ongoing challenge was that I had no life other than work. For five years, I kept a 24/7 schedule and viewed my work as a "calling," not just a job. I had few close friends, because I was seldom home. I had been so focused on making a difference that I wasn't making good choices in my own life. I was young, idealistic, and swept up in the headiness of all I was doing. I had unconsciously done the complete opposite of what women did in the 1950s; my single focus wasn't on home and family, but on career.

I asked a woman involved in the women's movement why the movement focused on the sixty-nine cents that a woman is paid for every dollar a man receives for the same work. She said that if the powers-that-be don't pay you equally for the same work then they don't value your participation in the same way; you don't need to be in the room where the important decisions are made. She added, "Once we get paid equally for our work, the rest will follow." I still held onto the belief that fairness in pay would follow hard work, but I was wrong. I worked hard, as did so many women I knew, but the pay inequities and lack of opportunities seemed there to stay. The glass ceiling was very real and the entertainment business truly was a man's world.

I thought I would stay in my position as Norman's executive assistant until *A Wrinkle in Time* was produced or until I had worked on another film under his guidance. I had turned down two job offers—one for a studio and another for a network—out of loyalty to Norman as well as the worry of losing my association with *Wrinkle* should I leave the company. Then, the inevitable happened. I found out a guy who had worked with us on *I Love Liberty* was hired to be another assistant to Norman, and my salary was the equivalent of sixty-nine cents to the dollar he would be paid. If it had happened two years earlier perhaps I wouldn't have cared, but by that time my consciousness had been raised. I was haunted by what that woman said about why the pay inequities mattered. The thought that Norman didn't value my participation in the same way as he did my new male co-worker was devastating, because my entire identity had been wrapped up in my job.

When I raised the issue with Norman, I had to face the hard truth about the pay differences between writers and executives. His new assistant was also a young writer who had written some of the funniest sketches in *I Love Liberty*, which was why he would be paid more. I saw it differently. I had been working with Norman for five years and helped create the special, so I had a hard time accepting the justification for the pay differences. Looking back, I had reached as far as I could go in my role with Norman, and he needed to work with a young writer on a new rewrite of his film *Religion* and the development of a new TV series idea he wanted to explore. I could stay and continue on as before, or find some other way to keep my connection to *A Wrinkle in Time* without remaining in a role that I had outgrown. I felt trapped; I knew that looking for a new job outside the company meant walking away from *Wrinkle* since the company owned the rights to the film, and I didn't want to give up my dream.

I have often thought I must have a friendly star hovering over me, because as I was trying to figure out what to do, an opening occurred on the Embassy Pictures creative team. With Norman's blessing, I was able to transition to a new position as vice president of Embassy Pictures and stay connected to *Wrinkle*. Working with my peers rather than someone like Norman, who had earned such an exalted place in the industry, was a new and welcomed experience. I faced all the same challenges women had to overcome in the workplace, but now there were more women on the team. We didn't just have one point of view but many, with different interests and different pools of talent to cultivate for potential film projects. I loved it.

The one challenge for me was to adjust to the role of film executive. I thought it backwards that young executives like me with little experience had the ability to pass on projects submitted by writers, directors, and producers with extensive credits, but that was the dynamic then and even now to a degree. Older execs relied on younger ones to have a finger on the pulse of what an audience wants and better relationships with new upcoming talent. It was a common practice throughout the industry and established filmmakers complained about it all the time. I had my first experience of being that executive when Herb Ross walked into my office.

Herb Ross choreographed dozens of famous Broadway shows and directed some of my favorite films, including *The Turning Point* and *The Goodbye Girl*, which earned Richard Dreyfus an Academy Award for Best Actor. Ross went on to direct a great classic of the 1980s, *Footloose*. I couldn't imagine what was going through his head when he had to pitch me a film project. I had about as much filmmaking experience as the tip of his ballpoint pen. He brought in a promising idea about a son who gets hit over the head while on a business trip with his parents. The son wakes up decades earlier and meets a much younger version of his parents and is ultimately responsible for getting them to fall in love. I thought it was a good idea and passed it up the chain of command.

We soon heard that Universal was in pre-production on something similar called *Back to the Future*. This episode was a lesson in how common it is for the same idea to float around and it becomes a race to see who gets the concept on the screen first. Another hard truth was that no matter what your credits, you were only as good as your last picture. *Citizen Kane*, often cited as the best film ever made and ranked number one on AFI's all-time 100 list, had been directed by Orson Welles, the man I almost killed escorting up a flight of stairs in my first year on the job. Welles had a few failures in his career, and by the 1980s, the only job he could get was as the spokesperson for Paul Masson wine commercials. The tag line, "We will sell no wine before its time," was a far cry from Charles Foster Kane's immortal word, "Rosebud."

I didn't think being an executive was very cool. We were often referred to as "the suits" that had little experience and all the power. I saw my job as a steppingstone to becoming a producer as soon as possible; I had to wear a suit but didn't want to be one. In my naïveté I thought that there was some mysterious checklist that all producers must have hidden in their desks. All I had to do was find this list and I would be a producer. Unfortunately, after taking lunches with other successful producers, having extensive phone conversations and asking questions of other film executives at many social gatherings, I found that no such list exists. One top network executive said that to be a producer, "You have to be a pain in the ass. They will finally make your movie because they don't want to have to deal with you anymore." That was inspiring. Another long-time film producer said, "A producer produces. You have to figure out how to make it happen." Great clarity. And this—one of my favorites—"Open a restaurant. It will take forever to get the film made and you have to do something with your time." Woefully, there was no magic wand. I also saw that it was far more difficult for women to produce anything without a male partner. It was okay to have a woman be the creative force behind a project, but the man was the one who dealt with the studio or financiers. As I mentioned earlier, we were conditioned to take the half loaf.

Thankfully, *Wrinkle* was one of the few projects the company was still interested in producing, so I convinced the head of our team to fund one more screenplay. My strategy was to let go of everything I had ever believed and just listen to what new potential writers had to say. No two approaches were the same. One writing team wanted to focus on the theme of love triumphs over all. Another wanted to write it as a story about a daughter and her father. Another was motivated by the evils of conformity. A few wanted to write it as a spiritual awakening. Writers often suggested certain characters be omitted like Charles Wallace, or Calvin, or Aunt Beast. The most jaw-dropping comment was when a film executive looked at me and said, "For the past two thousand years, Christians have said that love is the answer when we know that isn't the case; that has to change." No one spoke of the story's potential for humor or as an affirmation of life in the way that Norman and Madeleine did. All I could think of was, *help*.

The leadership of Embassy Pictures finally gave the go-ahead to hire a young writing team who had worked with Mel Brooks on *The Elephant Man*. Mel Brooks gave them a glowing recommendation, and they understood Meg's character arc. Their script had much going for it, but not enough to convince the company to move forward. When that screenplay didn't work, I tried to get the company interested in the idea of first finding a visionary director, then a script. That had always been Norman's first instinct, and maybe it was the right one. Mr. Perenchio, who was overseeing the film division, said, "Get one of the three top directors—George Lucas, Steven Spielberg, or Francis Coppola—and we will make your picture." I never thought in a million years that a woman would get the opportunity to direct the film. It was hard enough for a woman to get a movie produced and very few—maybe a handful—were able to direct small independent features.

Both Lucas and Spielberg passed and then I heard that Francis Coppola was interested so I flew to San Francisco. It never got old being in the presence of true excellence. Francis, the winner of five Academy Awards, was not just excellent but a master. A soon as I landed, I rented a car and drove to his vineyard near Napa. Today, his wine business is an immense enterprise—mixing cinema with wine and adventure—truly a one-of-a-kind operation. When I met with him in the fall of 1983, he lived in a beautiful Victorian home surrounded by acres and acres of vineyards that hadn't yet become this global wine empire. I arrived just in time to watch him make a delicious pot of spaghetti for lunch and afterwards we walked to a separate building that was his workspace.

After settling in, we spent hours discussing *Wrinkle*. He loved the book and all of its potential. Francis had an almost childlike approach to the story. He related to the kids feeling like oddballs, the awesome moment when a child discovers she can do something a parent can't, and the inherent mystery— who are those three women? It was fascinating to sit and listen to Francis speak not only about *Wrinkle* but other projects he was working on at the time. At one point, he showed me a work in progress—an outline of sorts for one of his films that had been mapped out on what looked like rolls of uncut butcher paper. I made a mental note for a new use for butcher paper, and left that day with high hopes. I couldn't wait to return to LA and share my good news.

Feeling very much like Dorothy returning to the Great and Powerful Oz with the Wicked Witch's broom, I entered Mr. Perenchio's office and said with a great sense of achievement, "We have one of the three directors!" I was flabbergasted when his response was a resounding no. He had just seen *Rumble Fish*, Francis' new experimental art film for teenagers. It was well received by teenagers, but not by Mr. Perenchio. How could he not want to work with a five-time Academy Award-winning director because of one movie? This was just another example of judging someone by the success of their last film, but he was the boss. The wind went out of my sails that afternoon and I felt like I was playing an interminable game of Whac-A-Mole and the mole was winning. I was back to square one—no director, no script, and no idea of how to move forward. On top of it all, my life was still only about work. It didn't look like I had a very promising future.

The one bright light in my frustration was Madeleine's unshakeable faith in me. I read a great quote by Abraham Lincoln which pretty much summed up what I thought at the time: "I'm a success today because I had a friend who believed in me and I didn't have the heart to let him down." I couldn't give up on *A Wrinkle in Time*, mainly because I didn't have the heart to let Madeleine L'Engle down. She was so important not just to me, but to so many others I had come into contact with over the years. I couldn't help but notice her admirers were almost worshipful, and I tried to convince myself that I wasn't like that. I was in her life to produce a movie. Despite my attempts to stay detached, over time I came to revere her and believed that the only way to get the movie right was to see the story through her eyes. It was through Madeleine's eyes that the book had its mystical, magical appeal to people of all ages and backgrounds. I couldn't give up no matter what.

In the spring of 1984, I was finally able to get an independent production deal with Embassy after the company went through a reorganization, which meant I was free to continue to develop the film on my own. I rented a small house in Hollywood across the street from my good friend Claire Townsend who had left 20th Century Fox by that time. She continually encouraged my pursuit of *Wrinkle* and urged me to do at least one thing every day—make a phone call, have a conversation, do research, something—to keep the project alive.

I found a way to get the most current draft to the then-president of MGM. His assistant called on a Friday and said he would read it over the weekend. I was thrilled. That is the call every producer wants; the head of a studio has your script for their weekend read. Not only that, but this was the president of the studio that produced *Gone with the Wind*, *The Wizard of Oz*, and so many of the movies made during the Golden Age of Hollywood that I loved as a kid. The thought that *A Wrinkle in Time* could become an MGM picture was beyond my expectations. Then I paused almost in mid breath—I didn't know whom to call to share the good news. There was Claire, of course, but I realized in that

With Claire Townsend on a break from writing

moment that success for me wasn't success unless I had someone to share it with. Monday rolled around and no call came. A week went by and then I heard the studio passed.

Claire suggested we try our hand at adapting the book, which seemed like a terrific idea since I had no means of paying for another screenplay or to go wandering the world searching for a visionary director. We even set about writing our own rules for what it meant to be a producer on our terms and access to daycare for all was on the list.

146

While Claire was sequestered away writing the first draft, Roz Wyman—the same Roz Wyman I had admired as a teenager—called to ask if I would come to San Francisco for a month and work for her at the Democratic Convention. Roz was the chair of the convention and wanted to bring the same kind of patriotic hoopla of *I Love Liberty* to the televised portion of the event.

It's one of those mysteries in life that it was Roz, in whose home I first saw Norman's name, reappeared out of nowhere to offer an opportunity that would recalibrate the direction of my life. I packed winter clothes, because I heard it could be cold in San Francisco during the month of July, and was on a plane within days. On my first day there, I looked out my hotel window and saw the Pride Parade and was wowed by the outrageous creativity and sense of fun. I had never seen anything like it. I put on my boots, my ankle-length skirt and sweater, and headed out to Moscone Center, the location of the convention. I arrived in a full-on sweat. It was one of the hottest days San Francisco had had in years, which was the first of many surprises that summer.

One of my favorite quotes pretty much sums up what followed: "The last step of any journey is the first step of an even greater adventure." As much as I thought it would be hard to top my journey working with Norman Lear creating People For the American Way, producing *I Love Liberty*, and learning from Madeleine, that trip to San Francisco proved to be an even greater adventure.

6

Finding Joy

I want to do everything there is to do
and then do it all over again.

PATRICK O'DELL

I was seven years old living in Houston, Texas, when I first heard the words "Democratic Convention." My father had just returned from the 1960 Democratic Convention in Los Angeles and regaled us with wonderful stories about shaking hands with movie stars. He was so excited that I became excited. Eight years later, I was looking down from the balcony in the International Amphitheater in Chicago watching the state delegations waving their signs in support of Humphrey's nomination. I noticed that the California banner hadn't yet joined in with the crowd. There were many in the delegation still in grief over the death of their nominee, Robert Kennedy, and reluctant to accept Humphrey as their candidate. A few minutes went by and someone finally picked up the sign and started waving it in sync with the others, which made me a little teary.

I was raised to be a true believer—hopeful in the promise of what could be when people came together to make
the impossible possible. I don't know if we are born hopeful
or if it's something we learn. If it's something we learn, I
definitely learned it from both my parents. "You get more
out of life that way," my father would say, and the years he
spent working for LBJ only reinforced that attitude. People
of my generation vilified LBJ for the Vietnam War, but I grew
up hearing about all the good he accomplished. From Dad's
point of view, Johnson tried his best to use his power to help
others. Reflecting back on those years, Dad said, "He was
someone who changed the course of history, and you can't
say that about too many people. He knew how to use government to bring about improvements for millions of Americans
in almost every aspect of life from reducing poverty to passing the 1964 Civil Rights Act, and from the Voting Rights Act
to creating Medicare and Medicaid."

The other difference Dad saw between his time in government and today was the bipartisanship between Republicans
and Democrats—not all Republicans and all Democrats, but
most. As he remembers it: "The fight for civil rights wasn't
between Republicans and Democrats; it was whether you
are for or against changing the culture of our society." I was
inculcated at a very early age to believe that the government
was there to help people. When Ronald Reagan said in his
1981 inaugural speech, "Government is not the solution to our
problem—government is the problem," I didn't know what he
was talking about. It was the complete opposite of everything
I knew.

By the time of the 1984 Democratic Convention, everything that I thought represented values to be admired—fairness, tolerance, inclusion—had been completely turned on its head by the conservative movement. According to conservatives at the time, Democrats were the source of every ill this country had faced in the last 50 years. When I got on that plane to fly to San Francisco for my month-long job working for Roz Wyman, I thought I had within me the same kind of passion for politics I had in 1968.

Working directly for the chair gave me a bird's-eye view of all that was involved in mounting an event of such enormous scale from the length of the bunting to be hung from the rafters to the scheduling of remarks. The politics of who got to speak when, the individual demands of the party leadership, the delegates, the mayors, the governors, the senators and members of Congress, the local officials, and the representatives from the various factions could be overwhelming. I had to learn how to manage three phone conversations on three separate phones at the same time. There were plenty of moments when I thought this was the craziest thing I had ever done—and if I survived, I could do anything.

It was an historic convention. New York Governor Mario Cuomo gave his riveting "Tale of Two Cities" speech that galvanized everyone in the convention hall. Women were elated when Geraldine Ferraro became the first female Democratic nominee for vice president. On the last night, Senator Ted Kennedy introduced Walter Mondale, the party's nominee for president, and the crowd went wild with excitement and solidarity. I was working behind the scenes that night handling the needs of visiting dignitaries, which included Frank Wells, the then president of the Walt Disney Company. The backstage area was also filled with political luminaries and the talent waiting in the wings to perform. Different party leaders wandered back to chat with one another, including the former governor of Arkansas and his wife, Bill and Hillary Clinton. I had met the Clintons a few years earlier in our search for the first president of People For the American Way. He turned down Norman's offer in order to run for governor again and won.

When Jennifer Holliday, the original Effie in *Dream Girls*, walked onto the stage to sing a glorious rendition of the *Battle Hymn of the Republic* I ran to find a spot on the podium to listen. I watched Mondale and his wife, Joan, along with Geraldine Ferraro and her husband, sway to the music in unison with the Reverend Jesse Jackson a few steps away doing the same. After the closing prayer, the Mondales stepped forward for the traditional rallying pose with arms held high in the air, while balloons and confetti fell and thousands of American flags waved along with the music. It looked exactly like the last closing moment I had witnessed from the balcony at the 1968 Democratic Convention in Chicago, only this time I felt differently. I didn't have the same passion for politics I did when I was fifteen years old. I couldn't connect with the words spoken that night or rally the same kind of enthusiasm and spirit that had always defined me. I wasn't the true believer I once was.

I had spent my entire adult life feeling like I knew exactly what I was fighting for, but in that moment on the podium, I realized that I had always put my beliefs into someone else's hands. My parents, Norman, and Madeleine were all strong personalities who had lived full lives before I ever came along. They had families and experiences that helped shape what mattered to them. I didn't know what I believed in anymore. I was about to turn thirty-two years old and had more in common with Madeleine L'Engle when she was in her early thirties than I ever thought possible. I had always assumed that Meg's yearning for something better was a developmental passage from childhood to young adulthood, but like Madeleine, I was a total Meg in my early thirties too. I felt just as insecure about my place in the world as I had when I was twelve years old.

Madeleine once said the sermons she heard at the local Congregational Church were joyless, and I felt the same listening to the politicians speak during that week. She was able to channel her need for an affirmation of life into her writing. I didn't think I would find what I was seeking in work. Matter of fact, I thought my singular focus on career and *Wrinkle* had made me the thief who stole my own joy. The question I asked myself that night was, Could I find a renewed since of purpose and meaning if I found someone to love and raise a family? Could I find joy living a life outside of work?

Betty Friedan's famous observations about the problem with no name ignited a firestorm of questions as women began asking about their role in society. One of the unexpected surprises in my life was when I had an opportunity to meet Friedan. She had dropped by the office to visit with Norman and we had a chance to speak—just the two of us. I said to her, "I know I'm lucky to have this job, but when you fought for these things you already were married and had children.

What are women my age supposed to do?" I was feeling what other young women were feeling as we approached the ticking biological clock—a very real pull between career and family. She told me I wasn't alone in my frustrations. As an aside, she ended up quoting me in her 1981 book *The Second Stage* in which she addressed the need for men and women to work together to redefine how to achieve success in both the workplace and at home.

It was difficult to speak about because women had fought so hard for the younger generation to have more opportunities, but something was missing—a new problem with no name now existed. Could we have it all? I knew very few young women in college who were there to get their MRS degree (in the olden days one of the main reasons to go to college was to meet a husband). By my time, the message was loud and clear that staying home and not having a career was a dead end. We all imagined doing something more productive with our lives. I loved my mother, but I didn't want to become her. I wanted to go out into the world, go on mysterious business trips, and do important work. My thinking took a drastic turn that night. I had spent years not wanting to be like my mom, and now I wondered whether I had been wrong.

It may seem strange to young women today, but I didn't know how a woman could have both a career and a family at the same time. It was an either-or question. There was no internet or cell phone to make it possible to stay connected to your children 24/7 no matter where you were in the world. Daycare was scarce, it wasn't easy to have a flexible work schedule, and if you were on an executive track then working from home wasn't an option. If a female executive went to her boss and said, "I need to stay home today because my child has a cold," there might not be a job waiting for her when she returned.

Seeing the Clintons backstage made me think of the first time I met them at Norman's home. He had invited Bill and Hillary to Los Angeles to discuss the next steps for People For the American Way and they brought their baby, Chelsea, to the meeting. I watched Hillary stay completely engaged in our conversation all while keeping an eye on her crawling baby. I had never seen a woman bring a baby to a meeting in my life until that moment. She made me think that maybe it really was possible to have it all.

On my way to the airport the day after the convention, I had to make one quick stop to meet with Patrick O'Dell, a producer Roz had hired to make a few videos to play on the giant screens in the convention hall during breaks in the program. I promised him I would stop by his office to see his demo—these were the days before sending a link was possible. I was genuinely impressed with his work. He was a talented storyteller and very charming. He was so likeable— I felt I had known him for forever. We started a conversation that neither of us wanted to end, and there was a moment when I actually thought he was going to walk me to my plane.

Patrick had a winning smile, a dry wit, and dark curly hair that had started to turn gray a few years earlier when he reached thirty. One topic led to another and I asked him to read *A Wrinkle in Time*. He called a few days later and we spoke for hours about the book, life, and everything else two people talk about when they start to fall in love. I had such a sense of inner peace when I spoke with him. Even my sisters remarked about how happy I seemed. I knew something was different because I played his recorded phone messages over and over again just to hear his voice. A few months later, Patrick invited me to join him for a weekend in Carmel to celebrate my thirty-second birthday that October.

He met me at the airport, and on the drive to Carmel, I felt so happy to be in his presence. When we explored the charming streets of downtown Carmel, I noticed that everyone else on the sidewalk looked like a blur of moving colors while every hair on Patrick's head was in sharp focus. As we sat together at a local restaurant, I wasn't sure if there were others in the room because I couldn't take my eyes off of his face—such a beautiful face—and I loved listening to his stories. They were a perfect blend of the familiar and just enough difference to captivate my attention.

Patrick had grown up in Visalia, California, a small town in the San Joaquin Valley, with two sisters and parents who adored one another. Unlike my upbringing, Patrick never had to move from school to school, but he did face a significant challenge of his own. He contracted polio when he was only sixteen months old. At that time, there was little scientific knowledge about the disease, so he was sent to Shriner's Hospital in San Francisco. A large room housed twenty children who were confined by huge ventilators and other machines performing support to over 15,000 per year. Many survivors lived the rest of their lives with deformed limbs and difficulty breathing. Polio was highly contagious, so not even family could hold and cuddle their child. Patrick's parents could only see him

Patrick O'Dell, summer of 1984

through a glass window and he would pull himself up in the crib and reach his arms up, begging them to come in.

Doctors gave Patrick the prognosis of being a "lifetime cripple," but his mother wasn't going to let that happen. When they took Patrick home, she started him on a course of a new possible cure, stretching his heel cord. She learned how to do it and worked with him on it until he finished high school, and no one ever noticed the length of his legs. Throughout his life, he was self-conscious about one of his legs being shorter than the other, but he was the only one who could see it; I couldn't even tell the difference.

Patrick was a natural leader. In high school, he always was president of his class and a member of Key Club, the boys who the teachers considered cream of the crop. He wrote beautifully. He sang the lead in the school musical. He studied Latin. He was an athlete. And he was up to mischief, quietly, on his own terms. The family spent their summers in the mountains of Sequoia National Park, where he learned to jump on and off a moving horse and loved to entertain the young girls attending a nearby summer camp. He had a passion for hiking in the mountains and would often say that is where he felt closest to God.

When his music teacher arrived for his weekly piano lessons, he didn't hide in a closet like I once did. Consequently, he could play anything on the piano, which helped him land jobs in local clubs in his late teens and early twenties to earn spending money. Those years spent strengthening his legs left Patrick with an empathy and kindness towards others that was very rare. He was also very proud to be sixth generation Irish and loved to celebrate his favorite holiday, St. Patrick's Day. After a stint in the Army, and then after writing and producing corporate videos for Kodak in New York, he moved to San Francisco and set up his own production company, Office of the Irishman.

He won me over that weekend when we walked along the cliff above the Pacific Ocean and I asked him what he wanted to do with his life. With a gentle sea breeze blowing, he turned and looked directly at me and laughed. He said, "Why, I want to do everything there is to do with you." When I asked, "What then?" Without a beat, he smiled and said, "*I want to do it all over again.*" Three months later, with a promise from

Norman that I could continue to develop *Wrinkle* on my own, I packed up my belongings and drove to the San Francisco Bay Area to spend the rest of my life with this sixth generation Irishman.

I walked away from everything I knew, not just for Patrick—although he was a big reason—but I wanted exactly what Madeleine said that night by the fire at Crosswicks: to know who I fully was. She was right—one of the most difficult things any of us ever have to do is discover who we fully are. It is also one of the things in life that is the most rewarding. I had never known the kind of love I felt for Patrick—deep, complete—someone who would be an equal partner in life. I remember thinking that if I had a daughter, I would definitely raise her to be a strong, independent woman, but I hoped she would never let her career interfere with loving someone like I loved her father.

I felt guilty and conflicted to want marriage and a family over career. I wrongly thought that I was somehow betraying the whole point of the women's movement. Had I become a cop out? A loser? Not tough enough to deal with the inevitable setbacks and difficulties making it in a man's world? Like Madeleine in her early thirties, I had to unlearn all that I thought meant success—to go back to that willingness to look at new ideas, to not be afraid of looking at new things in a new way.

I didn't initially understand the meaning of the seventeenth century poem by Thomas Traherne that Madeleine cited, "Surely Adam and Eve in Paradise had no more sweet and glorious apprehension than I," and lists all the pleasures of the senses. "But without further ado I was corrupted by the dirty devices of this world. Now I must unlearn and become as it were a little child again so that I may enter the kingdom of heaven." I had to unlearn the notion that my singular focus on work was not the only measure of self-worth. It wasn't easy. My entire adult life had been defined by deliverables. Phone calls to return by the end of the day. A packed schedule was a sign of an important person. "I can't do Tuesday at two, but how about Friday at nine?"

A few years ago, I read Maureen Murdock's *The Heroine's Journey: Woman's Quest for Wholeness* and it perfectly described what had happened to me. In the early days of developing *A Wrinkle in Time*, I often compared the story to the same kind of mythic journey that Luke Skywalker takes in *Star Wars*. George Lucas mentioned Joseph Campbell's book, *The Hero with a Thousand Faces* as a great influence on him during the development of the *Star Wars* saga. Everyone in Hollywood read Campbell's book to find Lucas' secret formula, including me.

Campbell wrote about the many stories told across all cultures concerning the hero's journey, stories that have been around for thousands of years. I was so conditioned to identify with the male in the great heroic tales that it never occurred to me that a heroine's quest would be different. In the early 1980s, Murdock interviewed Joseph Campbell and asked him about the heroine's journey. He replied, "In the whole mythological tradition the woman is there. All she has to do is to realize that she's the place that people are trying to get to. When a woman realizes what her wonderful character is, she's not going to get messed up with the notion of being pseudo-male." Murdock was dumbfounded by his conclusion and spent the next ten years researching the heroine's journey.

I immediately saw myself when I read Murdock's description of "fathers' daughters." She wrote, "Fathers' daughters are women who choose men for role models and mentors to validate their intellect, sense of purpose, and ambition. Everything is geared to getting the job done, climbing the academic or corporate ladder, achieving prestige, position, and financial equity, and feeling powerful in the world. Anything less than doing 'important work in the world' has no intrinsic value." What leapt out was the "and" that Murdock wrote after defining "fathers' daughters." She said problems can arise after a woman attains a certain level of achievement in a man's world and the question remains, "What is all this for?" This is what struck me that night at the 1984 convention. My earlier assumptions about feeling powerful were what I needed to unlearn; changing the direction of my life was not a reason to feel guilty but necessary in my search for wholeness.

There couldn't have been a more beautiful place to do that than Sausalito, California. It's a charming town in Marin County just over the Golden Gate Bridge and a favorite destination for international tourists. Patrick had rented a house high atop a hill in Sausalito that had a fabulous view of the San Francisco Bay. There was something new to look at each morning as the boats sailed from Angel Island to San Francisco or elsewhere. I loved taking daily walks along Bridgeway, the main street along the water where the tourists would often ask, "Will you take a picture of us?" Those sweet days in Sausalito were some of the happiest days in my adult life. When Patrick proposed with an old Irish proposal, "Will you be buried with my people?" I knew there was only one answer for me. We returned to Carmel early in 1985 to get married in the courtyard of a charming bed and breakfast. It was just the two of us. A short time later, we found out that I was pregnant with our first child and couldn't have been happier.

A few months into my newfound bliss, I received word that I was about to lose *A Wrinkle in Time*. Norman and his partners decided to sell Embassy Communications to Coca-Cola, which also owned Columbia Studios. It was the start of large corporations buying up media companies as a way to integrate their products and generate new streams of revenue. Studio libraries were seen as good investments. The libraries were like real estate holdings, only rather than holding onto buildings, homes, or land, they saw movie and television shows as properties that would increase in value. Embassy's library consisted of some of the most successful television shows ever produced and Norman, Bud, and Jerry stood to make a handsome profit. It also meant that if *Wrinkle* were sold to Coca-Cola, my connection to it would come to an end.

7

The Darkness

Descent into darkness is usually precipitated by a
life-changing loss ... filled with confusion and grief,
alienation and disillusion, rage and despair.

MAUREEN MURDOCK

I didn't know what to do. Just as my personal life had
become so rich with possibilities, the most important
connection to my professional life—the hope of producing *A Wrinkle in Time*—was about to end. It turned out that
I just had to be patient, which was something extremely hard for
me to do. My Aunt Bethlyn ran into Norman quite by accident
at a Hollywood gathering, which reminded him to check on the
status of *Wrinkle* in the deal with Coca-Cola. Bethlyn had been
with the Motion Picture Association for decades, first as assistant to the president, Jack Valenti, and later as a vice president.
She was someone with an iron will and a heart of gold who
taught me so much about navigating a life in the work world.
I often thought of her as my guardian angel and, it turned out, I
was right—big time. After a little research, Norman discovered

that the original agreement with Madeleine called for him to be involved with the film, which meant that the company's option to adapt the book for the screen couldn't be sold to another company.

Remarkably, *Wrinkle* became debt free. The purchase of Embassy included Coca-Cola assuming all the company's debts as well as assets. This was huge because all the development costs associated with the project added up to mid six figures. (In today's dollars, the approximately $500,000 against the property then would be $1.2 million.) Had *Wrinkle* not become debt free, I would have had to convince a new production company to reimburse Embassy that amount of money for me to set it up elsewhere. As long as Norman still controlled an option on the book, he made it possible for me to continue to work on *Wrinkle* without any financial encumbrance.

I was so very grateful, but I wasn't sure how this would unfold. Claire and I continued to work on our screenplay, but we faced the same problem everyone else did with the third act. The climax works in the book because Meg's transformation is an internal one that is exciting to read. The challenge was how to take that internal struggle and make it external, so the viewer could identify with it. We really needed a visionary director working with us to solve the puzzle. It was like staring at the brick wall in King's Cross Station and looking for Platform 9¾ that Harry Potter uses to get to the Hogwarts Express. You know it is there but can't find it. The project came to a standstill, but Madeleine continued to be supportive. She assured me that I was being very creative—except that rather than producing a movie, I was creating a new life within me. She said, "Just let yourself be." With her urging, I was finally able to let go of old habits in order to discover a renewed sense of what was worth fighting for—like gazing at a newborn baby for hours after our beautiful daughter Caitlin Elizabeth O'Dell was born.

With the birth of Caitlin, I soon found myself on a new kind of carousel reaching for a different kind of brass ring. There were days when Patrick would return home from work and I literally couldn't tell him what I did that day. For some reason, the door to the dryer was still open, the bed unmade, the top not put back on the pickle jar and the groceries not put away while I tended to the needs of our darling newborn. A new baby is like a vortex sucking all logic out of the air. I was forever asking myself where the time had gone.

Madeleine spoke about time differently than anyone I knew. While my nickname for *A Wrinkle in Time* was *Wrinkle* she often referred to it as *Time*. The word is sprinkled throughout the story: "He just does things in his own way and in his own time." "Just give yourself time, Meg." "She's busy. It's getting near time, Charlsie, getting near time." "We made a nice, tidy little time tesser, and unless something goes terribly wrong we'll have you back about five minutes before you left." Like the ancient Greeks before her, Madeleine measured time as in either *Chronos* or *Kairos*. *Chronos* is chronological time where deadlines rule the day. *Kairos* is "God's time," living in the moment oblivious to chronological time. Watching the happiness on my mother's face while she sang and played the piano for hours when I was a kid, or writing late into the night not knowing any time had passed, are examples of living in *Kairos*. Madeleine wrote in her collection of essays, *Walking on Water*:

Reflections on Faith and Art, "In *Kairos* we become what we are called to be as human beings, co-creators with God, touching on the wonder of creation."

I started collecting all sorts of articles about the theory of time, multiple dimensions, stars, and the questions being asked about the cosmos. I hoped they would help us visualize Meg's journey and update the science in the book. I still have many of those articles with titles like, "Score Another One for Einstein: X-Ray Data Indicate Dense, Spinning Objects Do Drag Space and Time," "Exploring the Eleventh Dimension," "Images of Hyperspace," "Man Scans the Heavens to Find Life (the SETI project)." I was really surprised to read about the discovery of dark matter. My collection now included articles such as "New Evidence Cited of a 'Fifth Force'" and "The Dark Matter Mystery." When I first read about dark matter, I thought about Madeleine, who had written about the Black Thing forty years ago and that now there is, in fact, something called dark matter in the universe!

My new way of using time was liberating, but it did come with a financial hit. Patrick's business was successful except for those months when he was looking for new clients or waiting to be paid by previous ones. I had to accept the absence of disposable income, which was easier to do in the mid-1980s compared to what young people face today. I didn't care, because I wanted to be a stay-at-home mom and know what that was like. I wanted to be emotionally available for Patrick, and I wanted time to develop good friends outside of work. As corny as this may sound, slowing down helped me become more aware of the beauty found in a star-lit sky, and more appreciative of the innate goodness in others. The stars were as bright and plentiful there in Sausalito as they had been when I had stared up at them with Madeleine on that trip to Crosswicks.

No one was more surprised than I that, after Caitlin was born, my commitment to *Wrinkle* only deepened. I now saw the story through a mother's eyes. The story captured all I hoped to teach my own children one day. I saw that the lessons Meg learns on her journey were ones her mother had learned a long time prior. The mother in *Wrinkle* has faith in the unknown, is patient and strong, and has unconditional love for her family. I now had a much clearer view of the Madeleine I observed at Crosswicks, and she was overjoyed to hear me speak about this newfound appreciation of the book.

I also finally had the time to cultivate meaningful friendships. Claire introduced me to the kind-hearted people who founded and ran the Mill Valley Film Festival in Marin County, and people who simply loved seeing films—not making deals—soon surrounded me. As time passed, I also made new friends while sitting around a sandbox watching my two-year-old make sandcastles. I met a young nurse who shared tips about the best foods for toddlers, and I was envious of her flexible work hours. I met a landscape designer, an occupation new to me. I found myself not only reading recipes, but exchanging the best ones for young children.

I thought I had lived a life that afforded me scope, but I knew so little about people who came from different backgrounds with different interests. Sitting on a bench with other moms at the local playground definitely created a level playing field in my mind. The one thing we all had in common was the love we had for our children and our dependence on one another to keep them safe from falling off the jungle gym. As one year rolled into another, by 1988 I was still hopeful about *Wrinkle*, Patrick had a steady flow of work, and I learned that I was pregnant with our second child.

As we sat down for dinner one evening that February, the phone rang. My mom was on the other end of the line, crying and having trouble getting her words out. She and Dad had just received a call that is a parent's worst nightmare—my beautiful brother Tom had been killed by a car while riding his bicycle on a local highway. He was only twenty-seven years old and had recently moved to Key West, Florida. It had taken the police several days to determine his identity because Tom had no identification on him, but they were able to use the social security number branded in his duffle bag to locate his apartment. Once inside the apartment, they came upon his photo album; an officer told my parents that he must have loved his family very much because the pages in the album were well worn. I was glad to hear that he looked at our family photos and knew how much he was loved and loved us in return.

Tom's childhood learning difficulties had become more serious in adulthood and he was diagnosed with borderline personality disorder. He tried his best in any social situation, even though within five minutes something would go haywire. He had a hard time sitting still or following whatever topic was being discussed—even as simple as the weather—and would inevitably say something off the wall. He was being treated at a hospital in Florida and had gone to court to

My brother Thomas Lyndon Hand, Christmas 1987

gain his independence. Someone at the hospital had some-how convinced him to move to Key West and live on his own. My parents had spent years trying everything to help him and were devastated by the loss. My sisters, my brother Chip, and I had done all we could to be there for him and felt such sorrow returning to our childhood church to say our final goodbyes to our youngest brother. I had such a hard time grasping that my baby brother whom I had protected all his life was gone.

Seven months after Tom's funeral, our son, Ben, was born and we felt that glorious reaffirmation of life. With a new addition to the family, we needed to move to a bigger house and rented a great place in Mill Valley, the next town north of Sausalito. The question I asked myself that night at the convention about finding joy outside of work hadn't been exactly right. I found that I loved what I did—finding good stories and bringing people together to make something happen—but I had not had a balance between work and a personal life. With Patrick, Caitlin, Ben, and a great group of friends, I had found that joy and wanted to return to work when Ben turned one. Like every working mom I knew, it would be a constant struggle between work and family, but doable with Patrick's support.

I heard through the grapevine that Fred Fuchs, the president of Francis Coppola's company Zoetrope and executive producer for the upcoming production of *Godfather III*, was looking for an assistant, a role that included developing new projects. Prior to meeting with Francis six years earlier, I had first met with another Fred, Fred Roos who was based in Los Angeles. Fred, or Rooster, the nickname those close to him used, had cast *The Godfather* and was one of Francis' longtime producers. Fred agreed to put in a good word for me, which led to an interview and, thankfully, I was hired.

The job required a daily commute over the Golden Gate Bridge to Francis's offices in the historic Sentinel Building in North Beach, a place rich in history. North Beach is like a little Italy with great restaurants, music, and the home of the City

Lights Bookstore, the hangout for the Beat Generation in the 1950s. Francis had bought the building in the early 1970s as the headquarters for his new company, American Zoetrope. When I started my job, *Godfather III* was already in pre-production. After twelve years of being in the entertainment business, I was finally working on a major motion picture.

If Norman was the pied piper of patriotism, Francis was a magnet for both new talent and well-established filmmakers. My days were always unpredictable, from finding a copy of a $400.00 check stuck in an old filing cabinet made out to Harrison Ford for his small role in *Apocalypse Now*, to running into Stan Lee wandering the hallways. Lee had stopped by to meet with Francis about adapting his Marvel comic books into films. It would take him another 20 years to make that happen with the right team. A day didn't go by when I wasn't learning something new just by being in proximity to Francis and the people around him. I loved all the back and forth on script rewrites and reading the notes from the studio executives. Francis's memos to them were as engaging to read as the script revisions. He wrote with such passion and determination; I realized how important it is to never stop selling your vision—even in a memo.

My favorite day working at Zoetrope had to be when the entire cast for *Godfather III* assembled at Rehearsal Hall 22 on Francis' Napa estate for the first read-through. No one was allowed in to observe other than the cast, Francis, and Fred. At the last minute, Fred whispered into my ear that I could come in to watch but had to sit in the back and be very quiet. There was such excitement, anticipation, and energy in the air.

Al Pacino, Diane Keaton, Eli Wallach, Andy Garcia, Talia Shire, George Hamilton, and the rest of the cast walked into the rehearsal hall chatting with one another and took their seats around a long table.

Francis sat at the head of the table and opened his script to page one. Everyone became very quiet and looked down as Francis read, "FADE IN: INT. VATICAN BANK—DAY." Wow. I swear I heard the trumpet play. While watching Francis work his magic, I found myself thinking about my high school drama teacher, John Ingle, and all the hopes and dreams I had as a young teenage girl. I thought to myself, "If Mr. Ingle could see me now!" I tried so hard to be perceived as sophisticated, serious, and conscientious, but on the inside, I was always a kid at heart.

While I had this great day job, I never stopped thinking about ways to re-ignite interest in *Wrinkle* and approached Fred about the possibility of Francis getting involved. Francis agreed to meet with us in his office on the seventh floor in the Sentinel Building to explore the idea. If I was a little nervous before the meeting, I really became nervous when we walked in and I saw all five of his Oscars on top of a cabinet. I thought of what Norman had said: When feeling self-doubt, focus on the *why* you are in the meeting and confidence will follow. My feelings of awkwardness melted away as I listened to Francis speak with the same kind of enthusiasm and visceral connection to the book he had when we met years earlier. He loved the inherent mystery—are these ladies good or evil? Is the Man with the Red Eyes a good guy or a bad guy? Most importantly, Francis really understood Meg.

News traveled fast in the industry and Fred and I met with executives at several studios. There were now so many women in decision-making roles who also loved the book and, once again, I heard, "There are no words to describe how much that book meant to me." Then I found myself in a very tricky spot. Since any studio would be optioning the book and not a script, I would no longer be in control of the film's future. Experience had taught me that the development process could be fraught with all sorts of challenges—a studio could lose interest and the property could end up sitting on a shelf for years.

I called Alan Horn to get his advice on next steps. I had respected Alan's counsel when we worked together at Tandem Productions and later at Embassy Communications. He might not agree with me, but he always listened with complete attention. Even though we hadn't spoken in years, it felt like it had only been minutes. He now had his own production company, Castle Rock Entertainment with Rob Reiner, after serving as chairman of Embassy Communications and president of 20th Century Fox. By the end of our conversation, he had convinced me to leave Zoetrope and work with Castle Rock.

His company would put up the money to develop a screenplay for *Wrinkle* with the intention of producing the film. I thought my interests would be protected working with his company since Alan and I had known each other for so many years. It also felt right to partner with him to get the movie made, because he had been the one who approved my initial request to go after the film rights.

A great byproduct of this new deal was a producer's development fee, making it possible for me to leave my day job with

Zoetrope and work from home. The timing was perfect, too, because our babysitter informed me a week before the deal closed that she was moving to Hawaii with her boyfriend. Caitlin had started kindergarten and Ben was two and a half; I loved that I was going to be home during the day.

Castle Rock moved quickly. Susan Shilliday (*Thirtysomething, Legends of The Fall*) was hired to write the screenplay and a female executive was assigned to oversee the project. Susan had loved *Wrinkle* since childhood and was an approachable collaborator. I found it troubling, however, when the company executive said, "I'm not interested in making a film for ten-year-olds." I was taken aback, because this movie had to appeal to the ten-year-old in all of us. Madeleine didn't write for ten-year-olds either, but she never lost sight of her ten-year-old self. The experiences she had in boarding school at such an impressionable age had given her an exceptional ability to capture a young girl's longing to feel valued. This is what made *A Wrinkle in Time* so unique—a great cosmic adventure written from a young girl's point of view. Within six months, Susan submitted a lovely script that accurately captured Meg's longing for her father and desire to find her place in the world. Unfortunately, the timing was off for Castle Rock to move forward. I don't know if it was the budget or simply the timing of which movies were getting made. Once more, the project stalled.

Shortly afterwards, I was confronted with a new obstacle that seemed insurmountable: Norman's film option on the book came to an end, which meant that the film rights reverted back to Madeleine. I couldn't afford to option it on my own, but Madeleine encouraged me to find a new home and then did something extraordinary. She promised not to sign any future agreement unless I was made producer of the film. That is how I became attached to *A Wrinkle in Time* as producer forevermore. It was an invaluable gift from Madeleine, and I soon set about looking for new partnerships to pursue. In my attempts to cultivate interest, I worried constantly about *Wrinkle*'s reputation as a project that lived in what is commonly referred to as "development hell." As funny as this seems now, I came upon a strategy after listening to a British commentator describe Princess Diana as someone with a history but no past. I began to answer the inevitable question, "Why hasn't this film been made?" with something like, "Oh, it has a complicated history, but not an insurmountable past—you mustn't let any of that get in the way of its potential."

I also entertained the idea of developing other projects with Claire, but that was difficult to do without any financing. We might be able to convince someone to let us have a free option on a magazine story or book, but we still needed to come up with financing for a script. My time with Norman had taught me how mercurial the business can be—a great idea today may seem passé tomorrow. He had developed a number of projects that never were made, and if Norman couldn't get his projects made, then Claire and I were facing a tough road on our own. Some of the reasons why I stayed committed to *Wrinkle* for so long were the enduring power of the story and the ever-growing popularity of the book. I was convinced that it could be made today or tomorrow or years in the future and would always be relevant with the

Hiking in the Marin Headlands with Patrick, Caitlin, and Ben

right team in place. A true evergreen property is hard to find, and this one was worth the effort.

I discovered during this time that the great benefit of finally achieving balance in my life was that when one side was on the downswing—like getting the film made—the other side was on the upswing—like our family life. There was nothing like the joy of watching my six-year-old daughter putting on a play with her first-grade class or getting a hug from my four-year-old son and hear him say, "I love you, Mommy," or a long lingering kiss from Patrick after we put the kids to bed. We loved being home and spending time with one another, or going on hikes together in the beautiful Marin headlands, or playing tag with the waves at Muir beach.

In August of 1992, the San Francisco Chronicle interviewed me for a story they were doing about a new social phenomenon called "burrowing." According to the information cited in the article, seventy-seven percent of American household members ages twenty-five to forty-four had a family with children and were spending most of their time at home. Richard Tarnas, author of *The Passion of the Western Mind: Understanding the Ideas That Have Shaped Our World View*, was quoted in the article.

Periodically a culture, or an individual, has to go through a certain transitional period of burrowing. A burrow permits new life to emerge from a cloistered, protected environment. This is happening right now. After an extroverted cultural movement that has lasted for centuries—the Renaissance, the age of exploration, the scientific revolution—now we're becoming aware of the imbalance and moral problems of that relationship to the outer world. We're turning inward to search for some answers.

My comment to the journalist pretty much summed up what I was thinking at the time, "People are re-evaluating their values. They're wanting to fill up their time with meaningful relationships, time to read, whatever you do to give your life more substance." A friend of mine, Carol Osborne, who gained a considerable following with her books *Enough Is Enough* and *Inner Excellence*, was also interviewed for the article and said, "For many of us, our family unit and our private pursuits are so rich now that a lot of what we used to call social activity just looks like busy work. There [is] a tremendous number of people not retreating out of fear, but being drawn inward out of an unfolding sense of excitement. There's something pretty exciting happening in the burrow."

And yet I still agonized over my inability to get *Wrinkle* made. I well remember an evening when I was seven months pregnant with our third child and broke down in tears. I felt like a complete failure. I had just turned forty and had been trying to get *A Wrinkle in Time* made for fourteen years. I didn't think it was ever going to happen. Patrick put his arm around me and asked, "What if you make it at forty-one? Will that count?" I looked at him and said, "I guess." He asked ever so gently, "Are you losing faith?" I wanted to keep the faith but felt less certain. It was Patrick who reminded me that it's easy to have faith when everything is going right. The real test is when everything is going wrong.

Two months later in January 1993, our youngest daughter, Meghan, was born and our family was complete. We named her Meg because I was resigned to the fact that the film might not happen, but at least we would have a real-life Meg. One week after she was born, Bob Weinstein, the co-owner of a small independent film company called Miramax, contacted me. He said, "I have to have *A Wrinkle in Time!*" I didn't see how such a small company could afford to finance the film, but I agreed to meet with him at the St. Francis Hotel. I thought it was a good omen given that thirty years earlier Madeleine had accepted the Newbery Award at the same hotel. On top of that, Patrick's great-grandfather's construction company had rebuilt the hotel after the 1906 earthquake. Surely, these connections indicated something promising.

As I listened to Bob speak of his passion for the book, I wondered if I sounded as over the top to others as he did. He was full of superlatives to convince me of his fondness for *Wrinkle* and his intention to get the film made. At the time, Miramax was known mostly for acquiring and distributing exceptional foreign films such as *Cinema Paradiso*, *My Left Foot*, *Enchanted April*, and *Strictly Ballroom*. They also had started producing small independent films on their own. I loved their movies, but their budgets were nowhere near what *Wrinkle* would require. He raised the possibility of Peter Jackson as the director since he was working closely with him on other projects for Miramax. I loved the idea because I was a big fan of his film *Heavenly Creatures*. "Jackson is a magician. He created his own special effects company and can make magic happen with little money," said Bob. Most importantly, Madeleine kept her promise.

Miramax got the option after they closed their deal with me as producer. Two months later, Disney bought Miramax. I had no idea how that deal would impact the future of the film.

The Peter Jackson suggestion fell to the wayside because he wanted to develop J. R. R. Tolkien's books *The Hobbit* and *Lord of the Rings* for the screen. Bob's next step was to start fresh with a new screenwriter and introduced me to one of his top executives, Susan Slonaker. Susan had loved *Wrinkle* as a young girl and together we set about soliciting sample scripts from agents and met with several potential writers. By the early 1990s, there were now many women writers to hire. We were very impressed with Linda Woolverton who had written the screenplay for Disney's animated version of *Beauty and the Beast*. *Wrinkle* had also been one of her favorite childhood books, and her commitment to the project was total. We met several times with her and left each meeting confident that she would capture the charm and humor in the story and she did. Unfortunately, there were creative differences between Linda and Bob. I could never figure out exactly what those differences were, but since Bob was the boss, we had to part company with Linda after the second draft. Linda would go on to write several hugely successful films for Disney including *Alice in Wonderland* directed by Tim Burton and *Maleficent* starring Angelina Jolie, but sadly, not *A Wrinkle in Time*.

After Linda left the project, Bob went radio silent. Miramax now controlled the direction of the film and I could do nothing but wait. I was ready to give up trying to be a producer after a particularly draining day taking care of our three young children, but I went to see a movie that changed my mind. As soon as Patrick came home from work, I left the kids with him and went to see *Wolf* starring Jack Nicholson and Michelle Pfeiffer. As I sat in my seat with my bag of popcorn, Diet Coke, and Red Vines, I wondered how long it must have taken to close the deal with Nicholson. What was his back end—his share of the profits? Did Michelle Pfeiffer get close to the same number, or less because she was a woman? How many rewrites were there? I was consumed with what it took to get the film made and then it hit me. I was there to escape crying children, not to wonder who got what in their deal.

I wanted to be transported to another world, to laugh or be scared or to cry—to be entertained. In that moment, I reconnected with why I wanted to bring *A Wrinkle in Time* to the screen. I wanted to do the same thing—provide an audience with an awe-inspiring experience that might bring a sense of hope and lessen the burden in their everyday lives. I had lost sight of my original motivation with the many setbacks along the way. I also recognized that trying to get *Wrinkle* made was a way for me to live my life in Northern California and still have some association with the entertainment business even if it seemed pretty negligible in that moment. There was far more to be grateful for than I had felt before entering the movie theater. Patrick had a new client, Caitlin and Ben were both doing well in school, and Meggie was pure joy. I walked to my car ready to face anything that may come my way—except for what eventually did.

On a beautiful spring day in March 1995, Patrick said he wasn't feeling well as we got Caitlin and Ben ready for school and Meghan for daycare. He had been to the doctor the day before because of a stomachache. He had taken a stress test and nothing appeared to be of concern. Around three that afternoon, he called to check in as usual and said he still wasn't feeling well and was going to lie down and try to take a nap. I told him he had to let up on the hot sauce he habitually added to everything he ate. Two hours later, the phone rang. There was a paramedic on the line. Patrick had collapsed on the floor of the lobby of his office building and the paramedic wanted to contact his doctor. Did I have a phone number?

I couldn't leave the house because the children were due to walk through the door any minute from their afterschool activities. A few minutes later, the paramedic came back on the phone. "I'm sorry. We couldn't resuscitate him." "What do you mean *resuscitate*?" I asked. "I'm sorry, but your husband is dead," he told me. I shouted in confusion, "What? We have a two-year-old! People who have a two-year-old don't die!" It finally registered what he was trying to tell me and I let out an involuntary wail of grief just as Caitlin, who was nine years old, and Ben, who was six and a half, opened the door.

I didn't get a chance to tell them about their daddy in a calm and quiet voice. They learned about him exactly when I did. We were all wailing. All Ben kept saying was, "But what about baseball?" He and his dad had been preparing for the opening of Little League season and he couldn't wait for the first practice. Despite his bout with polio, Patrick had been a regional champion shortstop in his youth and had taught Ben how to oil his mitt and place it under the mattress to shape it so it would be easier to catch a ball. They were looking forward to honing Ben's skills and going to the games together. Ben kept crying over and over, "What about baseball?"

I was late picking up Meghan and called to ask if she could stay a little while longer. I didn't know what to do in that moment after I hung up from the paramedic. Who do you call? Shock set in. I just remember trying to calm the children. "It is going to be okay. We are going to be okay." I called a friend who called a friend, and within an hour the house was filled with people. I kept looking around, asking myself why they were there. The minister of our church arrived and I overheard him speaking with someone about a service. What for? In that moment, I was emotionally disconnected from everyone and everything.

The next few days were just a blur. I couldn't listen to the news or carry on any conversation for very long. The only thing I could do was listen to the soundtrack of *The Lion King* over and over again. Who would have thought the music from an animated movie about the death of a great lion and the son's journey to replace him would be the one thing I wanted to hear? It was our family and community of friends that kept us afloat. Patrick was forty-seven years old and died on March 16, 1995, the day before his favorite holiday, St. Patrick's Day. His funeral was held a few days later and the church was packed with family, friends, and co-workers.

His best friend and Army buddy, Bob, captured the essence of Patrick in his remarks that day:

As you go through life, there are many people who
help you achieve what you have, but there are a
very, very few who help you become what you are.

Patrick came into my life—and I suspect it was for the same reason he came into the lives of so many others: because I needed him. I can still see him and Catherine with a very young Caitlin in a backpack, climbing the hills of Sausalito. Or with Ben on his shoulders, walking the sands down to the ocean. Or watching Meghan in a stroller as The Lion King parade passed through Disneyland.

Those were special times, times when Patrick was doing what he loved so very much: He was looking at life through the eyes of a child—with a great sense of wonder, and with a wonderful sense of imagination. He could simplify complexity, cut through confusion, and find the humor and the common sense in life. He encouraged us all to look beyond the immediate, to see beyond the obvious, to go beyond the ordinary. He taught us to try new things, to be good to each other. And above all, he taught us to smile.

Patrick had definitely taught me to try new things, to be good to others and, above all, to smile. Madeleine had lost her husband, Hugh, nine years earlier and tried to reassure me that Patrick was still very present in my life, "We don't know where they go, but they still exist," she said. Someone else said, "Your relationship isn't over, it will continue to develop just in a different way." I found this somehow comforting. Patrick wasn't gone, just invisible, but the tears wouldn't stop. I found myself crying in the most unexpected places: in the vegetable section at the grocery store or standing in the middle of

Patrick O'Dell, 1947–1995

Nordstrom looking for Meghan when she decided to hide in a clothes rack.

Death is the opposite of birth. When you give birth, the contractions come every few minutes until that blessed wail of a newborn baby. In death, the wail of grief is immediate and intense. After a while, you are able to go one minute without crying, then two, and soon you find you can go an entire day. The darkness we carry within us is often the most difficult to fight back. Maureen Murdock wrote in *The Heroine's Journey: Woman's Quest for Wholeness* that the heroine's "descent into darkness is usually precipitated by a life-changing loss . . . filled with confusion and grief, alienation and disillusion, rage and despair." I felt all of this and more, and found that grief brought with it a physical reaction as much as a mental or emotional one.

The most difficult thing I have ever done was to scatter Patrick's ashes on a hillside overlooking the Pacific Ocean. His tiny particles could no longer come back together and I became a woman with an amputated heart.

8

Darkness Can Be Overcome

So, stick to the fight when you are hardest hit—
it's when things go wrong that you must not quit.

JOHN GREENLEAF WHITTIER

A s far back as I can remember, whenever I was disappointed or sad, my mother would say, "God doesn't close a door in life without opening a window. Stop staring at the door that is closed and look for the window that is open." She also found a few lines from a poem by John Greenleaf Whittier and placed it next to my bathroom mirror:

Success is failure turned inside out;
The silver tint on the clouds of doubt;
And you never can tell how close you are;
It may be near when it seems far.
So stick to the fight when you are hardest hit—
It's when things go wrong that you must not quit.

Those sweet, inspiring words that had always helped me in my teenage years and early twenties fell on deaf ears after Patrick died. All I wanted to do every day the first year after his death was to sit on that hillside where I had scattered his ashes and gaze out into the ocean. I had told him only a week before he died that I wanted my ashes scattered on that very hillside if anything should happen to me. Now his ashes were those that had to be scattered and all I wanted was to be with him.

The daily tasks of living seemed impossible to sustain. Soon after Patrick died, my girlfriends created a month-long dinner drop-off calendar. Sometimes they wouldn't even come in but just ring the doorbell and the food would be waiting for us on the porch. Their small acts of kindness were a lifeline in the depths of my despair and created within me a lifetime of gratitude for each one of them. Caitlin at nine had an awareness of everything happening around us and was devastated by the loss. Ben at six was sad and angry, but marched in the opening day of Little League with his friends even though his heart was breaking. Meggie had just turned two years old and didn't really understand what was going on and provided relief from the pain with her smiles and hugs. We knew nothing would ever be the same again.

Fortunately, a moment came when I realized that I had to face my fear of living without Patrick for the children. To paraphrase Mrs Whatsit's words, I needed courage and I would do for my children what I couldn't do for myself. They were the reminder of the light I once knew within me, and the reason for wanting to find it again. My rock and close friend, Claire, was diagnosed with breast cancer in late 1994. She had been by my side during my transition from working in the day-to-day of the entertainment business, through my move to San Francisco, and while writing our screenplay for *Wrinkle*. We all thought the doctor had caught it in time, but Claire died nine months after I lost Patrick. She was only forty-three years old. Both of my irreplaceable pillars in life were gone.

I lived in two worlds: what people wanted to see—my ability to move on—and what I felt. I was adrift on the inside but knew I had to stay in the present for Caitlin, Ben, and Meg. A few months after Patrick died, I wrote a letter to my mother describing what my life was like:

Dear Mom,

You asked about my life now, so I thought I would describe a typical day from earlier this week. The day started on a promising note with a 7:00 AM conference call with a Miramax executive about a new writer they wanted to hire for *Wrinkle*, which was always a welcomed development. I listened carefully, called Madeleine's agent to relay the news and then realized I had let the children sleep too late. When I ran downstairs, I found Meggie still in her diaper and nightshirt, Ben upset because he didn't know what to wear, and Caitlin looking at her hair standing straight up, crying "I can't go to school looking like this!"

I promised Ben we'd buy new clothes that afternoon. I wet Caitlin's bangs, blew them dry in nanoseconds and loaded her gear into the car for her 5th grade camping trip. She would be gone four days and was feeling very uncertain about it. I scooped up Meg as is and raced Ben and Caitlin to school. Caitlin then realized she didn't have her pillow. I promised to get it and returned within minutes. When I came back Caitlin was in tears. She didn't have the right form signed, but mostly she was nervous about the separation from me. It hadn't been that long since her dad had left us and we all felt anxious about any separation from one another. At the last moment a few parents canceled and they needed help carting the gear to the ranch. I quickly volunteered and told Caitlin I would drive her so we could spend a little more time together.

We drove to the Walker Creek Ranch, a beautiful education site in Petaluma that was about an hour away. It was hot and Meggie would not cooperate. I couldn't stay at the ranch for very long and Caitlin seemed to settle in once we arrived. I was due back by noon for a conference call with the new Miramax screenwriter [no cell phones back then], so I had to be home by 11:59 AM. Meg took her nap on the drive back from Petaluma so she was now wide awake and wanted to sit right next to me during the conference call. She promised very sweetly that she would be quiet and played with Ben's Legos.

As I became more engaged in the conversation I noticed that she had gotten down from the chair. As you recall, my office area is on the second floor with a banister that allows me to look over and see the floor below. I searched for where Meg had gone all while listening to the writer speak about *Wrinkle*. Then I saw her drag the trash bag from the kitchen towards the front door and leave a trail of its contents on the living room rug—including a half-eaten roasted chicken and several coffee filters filled with finely ground used coffee beans. Once I got off the call, Meg came up to me and said, "It was a mistake." I asked her to "Please don't touch" and got the broom.

I picked up Ben at 3:00 PM and, as promised, took him shopping for new clothes. To my surprise, the shopping went well because I kept saying yes to every $10.00 "Gotcha" T shirt he wanted. At 6:00 PM the mom of Ben's best friend called to ask if we were going to the Cub Scout orientation that night. Cub Scout orientation? I had totally forgotten about the meeting. We arrived on time but then I realized I was sitting with the 1st graders instead of the 2nd graders where Ben belonged. Some helpful soul pointed me to the right room down the hallway. Meg cooperated for a while and Ben had fun making a totem pole. Her attention span didn't last long, because she wanted to play army with the boys outside. Never did I think I'd see my two-and-a-half-year-old daughter stick out her index finger and thumb and go "Pow! Pow!" She wasn't supposed to like guns. After everyone was in bed I picked up a *Scientific American* magazine to read about hyperspace and fell asleep midway through the first sentence.

Let's just say that Madeleine's definition of time as either *Chronos* or *Kairos* was insufficient. There was a third kind of time: when life is like a gushing fire hose and won't stop. That was my life. I had become the sole financial and emotional support system for my family, with little savings in the bank, inadequate life insurance, and never enough time to do all that was asked of me. Several people suggested that I not make any big decisions the first year after such a tremendous loss, so I gave myself time to think through how I was going to make ends meet.

I traveled to Los Angeles and spent a few days visiting with former colleagues and soon discovered it was not going to be easy for a woman to re-enter the workforce at the age of forty-two in 1995. I hadn't considered encountering ageism since I had always been the youngest in the room during my days working for Norman. That was no longer the case. No one said anything specific—they would get sued if they did—but I could see it in their eyes and the words they used. I worried about returning to LA because our emotions were too raw and the kids needed my undivided attention. I also didn't have the financial means or the stamina to deal with the ups and downs and long hours of the entertainment business.

I hoped that the screenplay Miramax was developing for *Wrinkle* would work, but it didn't. They brought on a talented screenwriter whom I met only once on that phone call with Meg by my side and was genuinely taken aback with his draft. He kept the title, the names of the characters, and some of the events, but he wrote a completely new story. I asked Madeleine to read it, and to put it mildly, she was quite irate. While she didn't have script approval, even Bob Weinstein didn't want to make a film that different from the original material. The good news was that I no longer carried around the fear that the reason the film hadn't gotten made was my fault. I had nothing to do with the script and it still didn't work, but I continued to believe it would work someday with the right team in place.

With no working script and no financial cushion, I realized I couldn't return to Los Angeles and live the life I once knew there; my career in entertainment had to move to the back, back burner. I began to appreciate that I needed to be closer to my parents and my sister Susie who lived on the East Coast. I was afraid of what would happen to the kids if something should happen to me. Or whom would I call in the middle of the night if one of them had a temperature of 103?

Just as I was trying to figure out next steps, my dad asked if I would consider working in radio. He was advising a small group of investors who were in the midst of buying a syndicated radio network. They were looking for someone to head their DC office, and while I knew nothing about producing radio, I figured producing is producing and I could learn. The skill set they needed was a blend of politics and entertainment, which I definitely possessed. It probably also helped that I had had experience creating something from the ground up as I did in the creation of People For the American Way. I had an interview with the fellow hiring, which was more like a gabfest than a conventional interview. We really hit it off and he offered me the job, which I saw as an interesting opportunity and a way to get to Washington, DC, to be closer to my family.

It was a tough decision to make because it meant the kids had to move 3,000 miles away from everything and everyone they knew, as well as adapt to life without their father. They were only ten, seven, and three years old, but I thought being closer to their grandparents and aunt outweighed the negatives. We set out in June of 1996 and I tried to make the cross-country trip a fun adventure for them. They really enjoyed seeing the Oregon Trail, Mt. Rushmore, and—thanks to Ben's curiosity—almost every trading post along the way. One moment, however, stands out as a metaphor for my life at that time.

We were driving through Yellowstone National Park and on the map—no GPS, of course—it looked like there was a turn off a few miles ahead that would be a short cut to our next destination. We took our time getting there so we could stop to see the moose and the buffalo roaming nearby. The kids fell asleep shortly after we reached the turn off and I began to notice that the road had turned to gravel and had become very narrow and winding. It was soon pitch-black outside and I could barely see where we were going. Worse, there didn't appear to be much to protect us from the edge of the road and the steep drop waiting below. If an animal had leapt out or a rock had fallen, we would have surely tumbled off, never to be heard from again. I couldn't believe I had gotten myself into this predicament. What I thought was a short cut turned out to be a fire trail. There was no way for me to turn around, so my only option was to keep driving forward. I told myself that we were not going to die, at least not that night, and not on that road. We finally reached a local highway and saw the sign for Cody, Wyoming. I pulled over just to breathe. We had made it.

Life after Patrick was just like that drive. We travelled a winding road, sometimes harrowing, and often fraught with unforeseen challenges, but I was determined to overcome the darkness.

That drive across country that summer was a first for my kids but not for me. When I turned five years old, my family drove from Texas to Washington, DC, in my parent's new Mercury station wagon. My father had started his job with Lyndon Johnson that fall and that trip became our new routine for the next several years. Half the year was spent in Texas, and come January, we drove back to DC when the Senate was in session. My mother would often get us to play the quiet game. Whoever could stay quiet the longest would get a quarter. I didn't always win.

When the sun went down, we would get into our pajamas and I loved to watch the cars outside the window. They looked like a string of pearls coming towards us, and a string of rubies moving in the opposite direction. Those trips back and forth between Texas and Washington, DC, followed by the move to Los Angeles in 1961, back again to Washington, DC, in 1965, and then back to Los Angeles in 1966 were the reasons I attended fourteen different schools by the time I reached ninth grade. The one thing I wanted for my kids was a stable home life where they wouldn't have to go to many different schools. I thought for sure this move to DC was a temporary situation, and that we would return to our real life in California within a year or two. As the saying goes, "If you want to make God laugh, tell him/her your plans."

My mother and sister found a small house for us to rent directly across from a good elementary school in Bethesda,

Maryland, just outside the DC city limit. Mom was prepared to sit in a lawn chair until the people who owned the house agreed to let us rent it. That's just like her. Both my parents and sister were supportive in numerous ways after we arrived. I couldn't have done it without them, because I wasn't operating on all cylinders.

As hard as I tried, my grief wouldn't dissipate. It was the physicality of grief that I found the most difficult. I had been so light-hearted, but I no longer had that same kind of energy, and I needed that for my new role as only parent. I felt like I was walking through molasses when everyone around me was bouncing about. There were many days when our new routine worked really well and then the days when it didn't. If one thing changed in our routine—someone got sick or a work deadline had to be met—everything was upended. Any working parent knows about these potholes in family life; it was just exaggerated and heightened as an only parent. Living in *Kairos* time became a wistful dream. I felt awful that my kids not only lost their father, but now their mother wasn't around as much as they wanted or needed. To this day, Meg remembers passing a note on several occasions to get my attention while I was on the phone. If only there were do-overs in life.

On top of everything was the strangeness of my job managing the DC office for the syndicated radio network. The network programmed a variety of shows to fill airtime throughout the day and had arrangements with several on-air talent. One such arrangement was with *The Hill* newspaper that covered behind the scenes on Capitol Hill. I produced a morning call-in show at nine with the young and very smart journalists at

The Hill, then another show back at our office on Capitol Hill at five in the afternoon with rotating hosts. It was intense, but I enjoyed coming up with topics and guests and coordinating all the logistics for two daily live shows. The intensity helped with the grief because I didn't have time to think about anything else but the topic for the day and wrangling guests. There were plenty of days when I didn't have a guest confirmed until eight fifty-nine in the morning or sometimes as late as five-fifteen in the afternoon.

Both programs were completely non-partisan and non-ideological and covered the hot topics of the day with guests from both sides of the aisle. The goal was to produce a balanced view of the inner workings of government. Attracting listeners required opposing viewpoints, which could erroneously lead people to believe that both sides were equally valid, although that wasn't always the case. We justified this approach by thinking we were educating our listeners, but there were times when it was really about creating high drama to attract a bigger audience. To my surprise, Richard Viguerie, the direct mail whiz who had successfully demonized Christians if they didn't hold the right political points of view, was now considered a great "get" as a guest. The beliefs of what were once considered the fringe of the Republican Party in 1980 now represented the conservative establishment in Washington, DC, in 1996. A lot had changed in the political landscape since People For the American Way had been created sixteen years earlier.

What I didn't know—nor did those at the newspaper know—was the origin of the radio network. I came to find out that Chuck Harder, who had led a feast-or-famine existence for most of his career and was primarily thought of as a populist and based in White Springs, Florida, had been the founder. Harder really went after the Fortune 500 companies leading the free trade movement in the 1990s. Pat Choate, an author and economist, had been a regular guest who shared Harder's anti-NAFTA view—the then new trade agreement between Mexico, Canada, and the United States. Both Harder and Choate worked tirelessly against free trade to prevent American jobs from moving overseas.

Once when Pat was a guest on the show, he heard Harder make a pitch for a watch made in America, and 5,000 watches were sold that week. Pat envisioned a radio network similar to the televised QVC channel that would sell only made-in-America products. Pat formed a corporation with a few investors to buy out Harder and kept him on the air to spread the populist gospel—and to sell the products. Harder's show was the main draw on the network, and over time, several on-air talents were added. Pat had hired me to run the DC office, which included a little time spent with the conservative political commentator Bay Buchanan. Bay shared Pat's anti-NAFTA views and had her own show out of the DC office. She was under the assumption that I had once worked for the author Norman Mailer and her face turned ashen when I told her, "No, not Norman Mailer—*Norman Lear.*" Many conservatives and populists saw Norman as the devil incarnate for his—and those of the People For the American Way—liberal views.

I didn't know what being a populist really meant until I went to White Springs, Florida (population then 600) to see

Harder's operation. He had bought a rundown but charming old hotel called the Telford. The hotel was the command center where he hosted his radio show. The people I met in White Springs were very welcoming, and I had my first taste of something called sweet tea, a Southern staple. I never felt so out of my comfort zone—and not because they didn't carry low-fat or non-fat milk. I love the South and Southerners, but their opinions about the country, the government, and the world were different from anything I had experienced up close. I discovered that a populist point of view appeals to people who feel that their concerns are overlooked by the establishment, and their opinions aren't necessarily based on facts, but feelings. If I *feel* it's bad, then it is bad, and it's very rare to convince someone otherwise, even with facts.

As a sideline, the Telford had the only restaurant in town. The townspeople of White Springs came there for their meals and to watch Harder host his show. Legend has it that when Harder first started his broadcasts, customers would often bring cash in brown paper bags to help him stay on the air. Harder's whole family helped run the company before Pat and his investors bought him out. His wife minded the books, and his daughter ran the shop in the restaurant and eventually ran the mail order business. I was in the heart of what would one day become Trump country.

Pat's group had great intentions—to raise consciousness about American-made products and keep jobs in America. The problem was that Harder had kept two sets of books that contained very different numbers on the sales of any merchandise. One book indicated a very successful business, while the other showed the debt he had accumulated. Pat didn't know the extent of the debt. Harder wasn't honest about the limitations of the technology he used to broadcast or to facilitate the on-air sales, either. I had my own experience with their technical challenges when we had then-Speaker of the House Newt Gingrich as a guest to be interviewed by the journalists at *The Hill* newspaper. After the show I learned that the satellite signal wasn't working so none of our listeners heard the interview. I decided not to mention this small detail to the gang at the newspaper.

There was also the problem of what Harder said on the air. He hated the government. His show was carried on about 100 stations in small towns across America, and his populism really appealed to them. Pat tried everything to get him to tone down his rhetoric and Harder would always appear to agree. Then the red light would go on and he'd say whatever he pleased. His audience loved it. There's not much you can do to prevent unwanted statements made by a host on a live radio show.

Despite everything, it was a worthwhile opportunity for me to interact not only with those running the network, but listening and learning from the listeners who called in. It was like stepping into a completely different world than I had ever known, and I was intrigued by what I heard. I had never understood the argument against NAFTA or why the listeners felt Washington had left them behind. Conspiracy theories tend to thrive in that kind of environment, as well as seeing the glass half empty. How else to explain the lack of interest from their government? Fox News launched the year I started producing the two daily talk shows, targeting the same audience but on a grander scale. Roger Ailes, the creative force behind Fox News, chose to inflame, validate, and affirm the anger that existed in the country rather than find a way to address it.

These callers were hurting. All the talk of retraining if their jobs were sent overseas meant little to them. The lives of millions of people and their families were being upended, and no one seemed to care. Our listeners were people with what Norman used to describe as "emotionally crowded lives." Every day, they worried about how to feed their families or pay for their kids' braces, or that the factories might be shut down. Some had overwhelming medical expenses. They didn't have the time or interest to read the op-ed page in *The New York Times*. I empathized with this anger at the world—that life could be so unfair—because I was feeling it myself. I was so angry that my husband had died. Why did my kids have to grow up without a dad?

It could be almost paralyzing, this rage at the world that I kept hidden within me, while acting on the outside as if everything was okay. "Stay angry, little Meg," Mrs Whatsit whispered. "You will need all your anger now," is an oft-quoted line from *Wrinkle*. Meg's anger is one of her strengths and vital in rescuing her father. A little later in the story, Meg is overtaken by the darkness. She becomes filled with uncontrollable rage and blames her father for not doing enough to save her brother. My anger was a source of strength until it wasn't. There is a fine line between anger and rage—not unlike the effects of the sun. With the right balance the sun makes plants grow and keeps us healthy, but when it gets too hot, it scorches the earth. I had a hard time finding that balance in the second and third years after Patrick's death when I had to accept the permanence of his absence.

I had something else in common with Harder's listeners. I, too, lived an emotionally crowded life. While my parents were financially comfortable and helped however they could, I worried constantly about money—how to make ends meet and how to pay for extras like my kids' braces. I didn't worry about a factory closing, but I had to look for a new job when the network switched direction. New investors were brought in and they wanted to focus solely on defeating NAFTA and were no longer interested in working with *The Hill* newspaper or presenting a more balanced view of government.

I became a part of the gig economy before the word was coined. Someone said of me, "Well, you don't have a real job," because in their view working in an office was a real job, while freelancing was not. I wanted to just shoot them right there. "What do you mean I don't have a *real job*? I have multiple jobs all at the same time." While it was impossible for me to participate in the day-to-day of show business, it was still possible for me to be a producer—just not of movies. I supported my family by producing events and outreach programs for nonprofits and the like, which kept food on the table and a roof over our head. The downside of working freelance is the uncertainty of where the next paycheck would be coming from. It was a very stressful time in my life. I had never imagined that life was supposed to be this hard. Wasn't I once voted Most Likely to Succeed? I felt like a complete and total failure.

I never expected to find myself curled up in a ball hiding in my bedroom unable to face the cries of my beautiful children and worried about paying the bills. Producing *A Wrinkle in Time* became a lost dream with no chance of ever becoming a reality. There was really only one option out of the darkness. I had to find the courage and confidence to face what needed to be done; I couldn't stay curled up in my bedroom. I thought about the oxygen masks on a plane—a flight attendant always instructs a parent to put the mask over his or her face first, then over the child's. I had to figure out how to find the oxygen mask and put it over my face so that my kids would thrive. I had to force myself to face down my grief. If I didn't work through this darkness, it would continue to consume me and I would live forever in the land of blame.

Blame was what I heard over and over again from those who called in to the radio shows: blaming others, usually the government, immigrants, or liberals. If you can objectify others and assign blame, then *they* are the problem. I didn't want to live like that. I better understood what Madeleine meant when she said it's not about the form of darkness, it's our fear of the darkness that has the power over us; the fear that it can't be overcome. Madeleine hadn't been able to change the fact that another war was looming when she was a young woman, but she could work to overcome her fear of it. I couldn't change the fact that Patrick had died and I had to work to overcome my fear of living a life without him.

In Maureen Murdock's book *The Heroine's Quest: Woman's Search for Wholeness*, she described the goal of the heroine on her journey was to "... confront her fear about reclaiming her feminine nature, her personal power, her ability to feel, heal, create, change social structures, and shape her future." I didn't want to accept my new normal for fear I would fail. I also missed my best friend who had loved me unconditionally and made me a better person. I had to learn how to love myself unconditionally and how to become those things that Patrick gave all of us so readily.

What was my first step in reclaiming my personal power? I had to stop eating pints of Häagen-Dazs Swiss Almond ice cream as a means to eat away my sadness for one thing. It was a dead end, and I had to find ways that were more productive and useful. Therapy was the best first step. Another was a daily walk with my dog rain or shine, including freezing cold rain or snow. That walk helped bookend the long process towards my self-transformation. Every day, I'd walk my border collie, Binx, on a lovely tree-covered path not too far from our home, sit on a boulder alongside a shallow creek, and say a simple prayer, "Help me find the light within me." When I closed my eyes, all I could imagine was a twenty-foot-thick concrete door that was slammed shut. I wanted desperately to find a way to open that door.

My walk reminded me of the walks I once took with Madeleine across the fields behind Crosswicks. On one of those walks, I asked her about the climactic moment in *A Wrinkle in Time* when Meg is able to rescue her brother with the words, "I love you." I wondered if that had come from a personal experience. She confided that there was a moment long ago when her then seven-year-old adopted daughter, Maria, was at her worst and Madeleine didn't know what to do.

At a very young age, Maria had lost both her parents and had come to live with Madeleine and her family. She was often very angry and in a moment of complete despair, frustration, and helplessness, Madeleine found herself saying, "But I love you—I love you." At the time, I didn't fully appreciate the heartache that Maria and Madeleine must have felt for very different reasons. Maria, who couldn't be reached, and Madeleine, who was desperately trying to connect with her. Now faced with my own anger and that of my kids, I held onto the love we felt for each other—it was going to be our only way through this fire. I was impatient with the kids and hard on my parents, my sister, and myself—no one could do enough to take away the pain.

What I had empathized most with the callers on the radio shows was their lack of hope. Without hope, it is impossible to believe that everything was going to be all right. I had no joy in my life other than the smiling faces of my kids. My therapist asked me, "What is one thing that brings you happiness other than your kids?" I replied that nothing made me happy other than my kids. She persisted that there had to be something, and I thought for a second and said, "Manicures—I like getting manicures." "Great," she said, "Go get a manicure today."

In the small act of allowing myself to enjoy a manicure, I realized how important it was to find little things—sometimes as little as finding a parking spot in a crowded lot—that made me happy. Then there was the unending love we felt from my parents and my sister Susie, who were determined to help us find joy again. Susie, the middle child of five, loves to have a good time, which was the perfect approach to life for three little kids. She would go all out at Halloween to get the kids excited about trick-or-treating around the neighborhood. Once she painted her face a sickly green and wore a black wig and an elaborate witch costume that was a huge hit. There were hikes along the C&O Canal, ice skating at the local ice rink, and helping us find a new puppy. Her presence was a constant reminder of how much fun life could be.

The real surprise for me upon moving back East was my mother's newfound fame. I had only known her as a stay-at-home mom and my dad's partner in life. When I moved my children back to DC and I was focused on providing for my family, it was my mother who had the blossoming career. Everywhere I went, people would inevitably ask, "Are you related to the jewelry designer Ann Hand?" There were times growing up when I had been asked if I was Lloyd Hand's daughter, but now—Mom!?

She chanced upon designing jewelry as a way to work through her grief when my brother Tom died in 1988. During a brief stay with my sister Susie at a resort on Captiva Island in Florida, she discovered stringing beads was very therapeutic. It required total concentration and gave her a brief respite from her sorrow. Her hobby became a business with her first commission to design a special commemorative brooch in observance of the renovation of the statue Freedom atop the US Capitol Dome. That commission set in motion what would one day be called her American Collection.

Mom was a child of the Depression and grew up with a deep love of country, having lived through World War II. Her jewelry designs were an expression of those long-held beliefs, and she transformed symbols—eagles, flags, and other cherished images of the best in America—into beautiful brooches, bracelets, cufflinks, and necklaces. In the early 1990s, when more and more women were assuming leadership roles, they were drawn to these symbols of power that had historically been worn only by men. Her designs were seen on the shoulders of first ladies, ambassadors, members of Congress (or their spouses), the spouses of generals and admirals, and young military wives. When Pamela Harriman, our ambassador to Paris, wore Mom's signature pin, the Liberty Eagle, on her first official trip to London the headlines read: "The Eagle Has Landed."

I spent time at Mom's store and was exposed to a cross-section of people, including those from the most prominent walks of power in the nation, to Gold Star mothers who lost their children while on active duty, to young military wives just starting out on their life's journey. As I engaged with them, I would occasionally hear about their own personal struggles— medical challenges, the loss of a loved one, or a financial downturn—and I listened to the steps they had taken to overcome their unexpected hardships. I once sat next to a retired four-star Air Force general at a dinner who had been a prisoner of war during the Vietnam conflict. He had been a fighter pilot and was shot down over water, barely escaping with his life. I said, "Oh, you mean like Tom Cruise in *Top Gun*?" He looked at me, paused a moment and then said, "Tom Cruise is an actor. I'm the real thing." Talk about a reality check.

Thankfully, he forgave me for that ridiculous comment. He went on to describe how he had to learn to lower his pulse rate when he and other men were prisoners held in a small tin hut where the temperature could get to 110°. Listening to him and to so many others in public service, I was faced with how limited my world view had been. I had spent a lifetime thinking filmmaking was the best way to make a difference, never giving enough thought to the people who spent their lives making personal sacrifices so I could enjoy my life. My consciousness was raised in an entirely new way.

Little bit by little, our lives did improve, although we didn't get to the place of "living happily ever after." Dealing with the loss of someone we loved didn't happen like that for us. It was an ongoing effort as we learned better coping skills. I made many bad decisions and wrong turns, and argued too often with the kids until we figured out what worked best for us—listening well, learning how to communicate, and trusting the love we had for one another. It took hundreds of little moments that made it possible for joy to eventually fill our home. I found that to be liberated is not to be defined by any one thing—not a career, one's background, or motherhood—but to embrace the many layers of what makes you *you*. A sense of humor didn't hurt either.

Learning to live a life with grace and understanding was a more inclusive and hopeful way of being in the world. We got to the other side of the fire with the love we received from our family and friends, and the lessons I learned early in life about resilience. Learning how to be flexible and weathering fourteen different schools turned out to be a good thing. It probably helped that I had read a book when I was ten years old that taught me that darkness exists and that it can be overcome. I certainly didn't know it then, but the fighters Madeleine wrote about in *Wrinkle* each had their own encounters with darkness.

Leonardo da Vinci had been a promising artist in his twenties, but the only work he could get was painting cadavers and a few projects for the duke of Milan that didn't go well. Madame Curie lived in poverty for seven years while studying physics before she went on to become the first woman awarded the Nobel Prize. Beethoven lost his hearing and created some of his greatest works while completely deaf. Mahatma Gandhi was discriminated against for being an Indian immigrant and sent to jail multiple times in his resistance to social and political injustice. Einstein had trouble getting a job once he graduated from college, and his father thought he was a complete failure. Bach was orphaned at the age of ten and had twenty children, but only nine outlived him.

Patrick had been right: It's easy to have faith when everything is going right. The *real* test is when everything is going wrong. After a lot of hard work facing what I didn't want to face, I was finally able to open that twenty-foot-thick door and walk through it to the other side. While adapting *A Wrinkle in Time* for the screen seemed unattainable, I convinced myself that I had a career in the entertainment business as long as I hung on to the hope of the movie getting made one day.

Four years after Patrick died, the phone rang late one night. Bob Weinstein from Miramax called to ask what I thought about making *Wrinkle* for television. Television! We could project it from the moon as far as I was concerned. He just told me that my dream was alive.

9
Childlike Wonder

If the book will be too difficult for grown-ups,
then you write it for children.

MADELEINE L'ENGLE

There is much joy in learning something or someone you thought was lost is found. As a child, I
always felt a sense of loss when my dad was away
on one of his business trips and was elated upon his return.
All five of us would pile into our family station wagon with
Mom at the wheel and drive to the Los Angeles airport to
greet him. We'd run—or walk really fast—to the gate and
passersby would hear five little kids squealing with delight,
"Daddy, Daddy!" the moment we saw him walk through the
passageway. Our shouts of joy were followed by a mad dash
to get that first hug. I knew Meg Murry's yearning to have her
father home. I felt it often in my own life.

I had been hooked on the story the moment Meg learns
that her missing father is alive. I kept reading to discover if

she found him. I loved the suspense, the thrill of traveling—tessering—through multiple dimensions, the excitement of Meg finding her father, and the pure joy when Meg discovers the secret weapon against the evil force. I loved how the book inspired my imagination.

My goal was to capture on screen those same feelings of unadulterated joy I knew as a kid. Madeleine once said, "You have to write the book that wants to be written. And if the book will be too difficult for grown-ups, then you write it for children." This was the key I came to understand in my conversations with her. An important reason that Madeleine had received those twenty-six rejections was because adults didn't think the young reader would understand the themes in the book. Madeleine said, "The editors kept asking what age group was it for. They mistakenly thought that because the mathematics was too difficult for grown-ups it would be too difficult for children."

John Farrar, who had eventually agreed to publish the book, gave it to a librarian to read for her advice. He shared the librarian's response with Madeleine, "This is the worst book I have ever read. It reminds me of *The Wizard of Oz.*" Farrar advised Madeleine to not get her hopes up, "Please don't be upset if it doesn't sell, because we don't expect it to." Clearly, many of the adults who initially rejected the book possessed what Madeleine once described as the "restrictive fears that frighten an unimaginative adult world." I learned early from her that we had to maintain the childlike sense of wonder inherent in the story. It was the best way to drive home its underlying themes.

Almost everyone I ever talked to about *Wrinkle* would become very animated—almost childlike—describing their feelings for the book, and those were the feelings I hoped to replicate in the movie. Bob Weinstein had been as enthralled with the childlike sense of wonder as anyone else, but he had grown weary of the development process, which was why I was so surprised by his phone call. The switch to a television format came about because he had started a small independent unit within Miramax called Dimension Films, and he thought *Wrinkle* could be produced as a TV film under this new banner. After twenty years of trying to get it made as a motion picture, I was open to anything.

In what seemed like minutes, I was introduced to Billy Campbell who was then president of Miramax Television. Billy also supervised Bob's projects with Dimension and was directed by his boss to get the television movie made. Billy immediately set about finding a more seasoned producer to work with me on the project and asked if I had ever met a producer named Jordan Kerner. I laughed because Jordan had been a few years ahead of me in high school and I had given the nominating speech for him when he ran for student body president. Alas, he had lost that election but went onto become a very successful producer in the entertainment business. Yes, I knew Jordan Kerner and looked forward to working with him. Once Jordan came on board, I received a producer's development fee that enabled me to focus full time on getting the film off the ground.

Jordan read Susan Shilliday's script from my days with Castle Rock. He really liked it, and rather than spending time to look for a new writer, Bob decided to buy the script. As soon as Susan agreed to join our team, we were that much closer to a green light. The only catch was that to get a bigger budget we had to stretch what I had always seen as a two-hour movie into a 4-hour miniseries and produce it in Canada for the tax credits. The structure for a miniseries is very different than a film and would require Susan to add many more scenes and new characters to adapt the screenplay for this new format.

I was shocked when the network said we had to cut the haunted house scene in the book for budgetary reasons. This key scene has potential for fun and mystery and is where Meg meets a second mysterious old woman and Meg's classmate, Calvin, who joins the quest to find Dr. Murry. I soon began to understand that the four hours for the miniseries didn't include scenes that would require a bigger budget. I was so green, I didn't appreciate how the inadequate budget would impact every choice we made for the miniseries—the locations, cast, special and visual effects, post production, and marketing.

The good news was that the network became more and more invested in the project even though the script wasn't where it needed to be. We had to hire as many Canadian cast and crewmembers as possible to receive tax credits, and we also faced a looming actor's strike—a "normal" situation that most projects encounter in one way or another. Jordan rightfully said, "We have to make it work when the planets are in alignment because it doesn't happen that often."

We were soon looking for a director. Jordan had always admired John Kent Harrison's made-for-television film *What the Deaf Man Heard* and suggested we meet with him for the project. I felt it was important for John and Madeleine to meet, but she was too ill to travel west and John was too busy to travel east, so I arranged a conference call between the two of them. I took the train to NY to be with Madeleine, and afterwards she turned to me and said, "I like him. He'll be good." Before the call, my shoulders had been hunched up around my ears with worry about everything, especially how Madeleine would react to the director. When she said that, I finally let my shoulders relax. I took a deep breath and thought to myself that this was going to work.

At last, *A Wrinkle in Time* was going to be made into a movie—or a miniseries, anyway. I arrived in Vancouver in late spring 2000 with Meghan, who was then seven years old. It was too close to the end of the school year for Caitlin and Ben to take time off from school, but they were able to come for a visit. We had a very caring woman who lived with us and I knew they would be in good hands with her, and my parents lived about five minutes away. Meggie had often been carted around to accommodate her older brother and sister's sched-ules, and now she had me all to herself. We made the best of this special mother-daughter time and took bike rides around Vancouver, had great sushi, and discovered chocolate and banana crepes. Since Meg was able to attend school with the other kids on the set, she was always nearby during the day.

The moment I met John Kent Harrison in person, I immedi-ately understood why Jordan was so fond of him and his work. He had a commanding presence and exuded both strength and kindness. Set construction was underway by the time I arrived, as were hiring the crew and scouting locations. John invited me to sit in on several casting sessions, and there was a moment when I was transported back to my teenage years dreaming about attending Julliard to become an actress. Julliard was considered the best performing arts school in America; both Robin Williams and Christopher Reeve went there, among many others. I hadn't auditioned because I didn't think I'd get in. Now I was meeting actors who had and wondered if the roles would have been reversed if I had had the courage to audition.

Filmmaking is without a doubt one of the most collaborative art forms, and collaboration isn't always easy—creative tensions are inevitable as you navigate the process to find what works best for the project under complex circumstances. I tried to be a good collaborator and to pick my battles. There were two major elements I fought to get right: the childlike wonder of the story and the crisis-filled emotional rollercoaster of young female adolescence. Everyone I ever worked with on the adaptation had the same desire to capture that sense of awe when they first approached the material, but as the initial passion shifted into development mode, it would easily get derailed. I understood the temptation to want to develop themes that would resonate with adults but never wanted to compromise again for young people in the audience.

Meg, Charles Wallace, and Calvin didn't go on a bus ride to Cincinnati with their eccentric aunts; they embarked on a grand cosmic journey with otherworldly energy forces and discovered the mysteries of the universe. Part of the book's allure is how it inspires the imagination; I hoped to produce a film that did the same thing. We had to make the most of all that was special and unique to their galactic adventure. It was the time spent with Norman and Madeleine that helped me to be so tenacious. Every one of Norman's television series dealt with tough social issues, but they were outrageously funny and it was in the middle of a great belly laugh that the audience internalized the seriousness of a topic. It was the same with Madeleine. *Wrinkle* is filled with all sorts of serious themes, but it was the childlike fascination with the unknown universe that reached people of all ages.

I had always loved how Madeleine depicted the emotional rollercoaster of a young girl on the threshold of adolescence. It wasn't just one emotion but a dozen, and all at the same time. That time in my own life was filled with mixed emotions— raging hormones is the common description. One moment I was shy and unsure what to say in a social situation, easy to anger at something that seemed unfair and then quick to dry my eyes after crying over some catastrophe so I could go outside to play kickball.

My young teenage angst was real but so was my willingness to drop everything when the doorbell rang and go with my friends into Westwood Village for a movie and an ice cream cone. It wasn't always serious and dark, but full of impatience and curiosity as well. The one bright spot during those years was that no matter how difficult my young crisis-filled life seemed, my dad had a way of making everything better. He believed in me when I didn't believe in myself. He didn't teach me math shortcuts like Meg's father taught her, but he encouraged me to express my opinion and explain why I believed what I did.

Midway through the television production, it hit me how much the deep bond between Meg and her younger brother, Charles Wallace, continued to remind me of my own relationship with my youngest brother, Tom. Without realizing it, part of my drive to get the project made was to honor Tom after his death. When I was a young girl and read "Charles Wallace was still young enough that Meg could reach him and he could escape the clutches of the It," I thought if I loved Tom enough he could escape the challenges he faced. In the climactic moment, when Meg finally rescues her brother, she says, "Charles Wallace, you are my darling and my dear and the light of my life and the treasure of my heart, I love you." Tom had loved it when I called him the light of my life and the treasure of my heart. The very last letter he wrote to me ended with "You are the light of my life and the treasure of my heart." I never could rescue Tom from his personal darkness and bring him home, but I could produce a movie about a sister who did. I hoped that someone else would also benefit from watching a sister rescue her brother when that might not be possible in real life.

As the weeks of production passed, I became more and more concerned that we were losing the mystery, charm, and sense of awesomeness of the universe. Sometimes it felt that it had been sacrificed for a more downbeat vision that was devoid of the fantastical. The moments when we should be taking in the wonders of the cosmos seemed often to be rushed through—almost an afterthought. This was certainly true when I saw a prop master use a folding metal chair for Calvin when he is imprisoned and separated from Meg. A folding metal chair? On a planet in another galaxy far, far away?

The entire cast and crew did their best, but we were constantly dealing with problems whose solutions required a bigger budget. The answer inevitably became, "We will fix it in post." The lack of a proper budget hurt us the most with visual effects, even though talented people tried to make magic happen with very limited resources. We never could get the tessering effect right, and we tried so many ways to tackle the metamorphosis of Mrs Whatsit into creature Whatsit. To no one's surprise, when Bob Weinstein saw the first cut of the miniseries he asked, "Where is *A Wrinkle in Time*?"

Making the story a miniseries was an example of fitting a square peg into a round hole. The changes and additions that had been made to meet the expanded time requirements of a four-part miniseries resulted in losing the original story everyone loved. After John and then Jordan showed their edited versions to Bob, he allowed my friend, collaborator, and former Miramax executive, Susan Slonaker and me a turn in the editing room. Susan had had invaluable experience on the foreign films Miramax acquired working with directors to make the films more accessible to American audiences. She had even worked on one of my all-time favorite foreign films, *Cinema Paradiso*.

I learned a great deal from her—especially when she shared her experience working with the director of *Pelle the Conqueror*, Bille August. Susan brought a scalpel approach to the challenge of audiences not responding well to *Pelle*, concentrating on elements of the film that August particularly wanted audiences to "get." She first discussed the film's story, characters, and themes with him. What did he want audiences to feel and to take away from the experience? Next, she had to ascertain why audiences weren't getting what he wanted. What were the elements still in the film that were getting in the way of the audiences' enjoyment? The real value Susan and her colleagues at Miramax brought was to serve as a catalyst to step back and see *Pelle* through new eyes. Bille August was pleased with the revised version, and the film went on to win many awards, including the Academy Award for Best Foreign Film.

My hope was Susan could bring that scalpel to *Wrinkle*. Our efforts proved helpful. We worked for weeks with the editor to make some scenes more mysterious, including the opening and when the children learn about the dark forces in the universe from the Happy Medium. We also did what we could with the footage we had to add more suspense on the evil planet, Camazotz. When Bob saw the cut he agreed to bring someone else on board to shoot new scenes in Canada. We would now see the kids as they entered the Happy Medium's cave in awe of what they saw. The action in Central Central, the home of the Man with the Red Eyes, was more suspenseful, and their tesser home was more glorious. I also asked Bob to float the idea with ABC that this not be aired as a miniseries, but as a one-night event. We needed to remove much of what had been invented for the miniseries to restore the original story. Thankfully, ABC agreed to the change, and the miniseries aired as a film. It went on to win Best Feature at the Toronto Children's Film Festival, but I knew it could have been better.

With Miramax executive and my close friend,
Susan Slonaker, and Madeleine

I couldn't let go of the sinking feeling that this version didn't capture what had inspired me all those years ago. I may have first fallen in love with the story as a child, but watching my children grow up made me appreciate it all over again. I watched them experience many of the challenges Meg, Calvin, and even Charles Wallace face, and I saw the enduring power of the story in my own family. There was something so special in the tale that I couldn't give up until I got it right. It had to work. I needed it to work, and my hopefulness came from that need. My children helped me see something about this story I had never focused on before—the cathartic experience

Wrinkle provides for children, including mine—who can't bring their fathers home. I knew my understanding of darkness and overcoming my fear was crucial after Tom and Patrick's deaths, but I had never thought about how much children who are separated from their fathers due to divorce or death could also benefit from the story.

My daughters loved the remake of *Parent Trap* and always grew excited when the twin raised by her mother meets her dad for the first time. She can't stop saying the word *dad*: "Ok, Dad," "Yes, Dad," "Whatever you say, Dad." Her father turns to ask if everything is okay and the audience gets that she just loves saying the word "dad" because she had never been able to say it before. I watched my own daughters mouth the word "dad" while watching the film. They taught me that a movie about a young girl reuniting a broken family was a much-needed story in a time of so many broken families.

As much as it goes against my grain to admit, we were a broken family. No matter how hard I tried, I could never fully comprehend the impact losing their dad had on my children, especially since I had a close relationship with my own. The therapist I consulted soon after Patrick's death said that they would reprocess their grief in different ways at different developmental stages, and that is what happened. I was also told that the age at which they were when they lost their father would drastically affect how they dealt with it the rest of their life, and I found that also to be true. What I didn't understand, or maybe didn't want to understand, was how much the decision to move across country resulted in a secondary form of grief.

Their friends in California had known their dad, but their new classmates couldn't comprehend what they were feeling—their suffering and loss—which made everything so much harder. Early adolescence, a time for exploring friendships, learning from others, and relying less on your parents, became a more complicated period for both Caitlin and Ben. Meg had it easiest when it came to social development with her peers because she had been so young when she lost her dad. I had a false sense that Meg was doing the best, and at the beginning she was, but as she grew older and reprocessed the loss of her dad, and had to deal with the repercussions of her older brother and sister's sadness, it became hard for her too. I wasn't the only one who made sacrifices for the sake of our family—so did my children. I once had wondered what the word "resilience" meant when I first read *A Wrinkle in Time*. Watching my children's resilience in the face of such darkness gave me the answer in a deep and profound way. Childhood resilience is indeed a gift.

It was Ben's love for the book *Harry Potter and the Philosopher's Stone* that helped me see a possible next step for *Wrinkle*. He was crazy excited about this book, and I had never heard Ben express such love for reading. When I learned that J. K. Rowling was scheduled to speak at the National Press Club, I took Ben out of school so he could meet her and she could sign his copy of the book. We must have been the first in line to see the movie in November 2001, and I immediately thought *Wrinkle* had the potential to be another *Harry Potter*—a big, wondrous adventure from a young girl's point of view—but how was I going to make that possible? Two years after the TV version of *Wrinkle* aired in the United States, I saw an opportunity to get it made as a film and grabbed it.

10

Like vs Equal

Like and equal are not the same thing at all.

MEG MURRY, *A WRINKLE IN TIME*

I n March 2005, it was announced that Disney and Miramax were ending their business arrangement. Disney bought out Miramax's considerable library of films except for those under the Dimension Films banner—the film unit run by Bob Weinstein. The TV version of *Wrinkle* had been a Miramax and Dimension TV production, and I was concerned that any hope of getting it made as a motion picture would be nil if I couldn't persuade Disney to take the property in the divorce.

I don't recall how, but I found a way to meet with then chairman of Walt Disney Pictures, Dick Cook, in the fall of 2005. He had started his career at Disney in 1970, working on the Jungle Cruise ride at Disneyland. By 2005, he was one of the most admired and respected top executives at the company. Only Dick Cook could hear my idea about remaking *Wrinkle* as a film and not call me crazy. He knew of the book and promised to make sure the studio took the property in the settlement. I remained hopeful that this new development would lead to something positive, but I had to focus my attention on ways to make ends meet at home in the meantime. I joined a public relations firm in Washington, DC, and continued producing events for corporations and institutions, forever juggling calls on the film and staying available for my three kids with one in middle school, one in high school, and one in college.

I knew that if I ever got a chance to produce the film that living in Washington, DC, posed significant problems. I would need a partner who had more experience producing a big-budget film, so I reached out to Cary Granat. Cary had been head of production for Dimension Films (*Spy Kids*), and co-founded Walden Media (*Chronicles of Narnia: The Lion, the Witch, and the Wardrobe*). Even though we had never met, I knew he was a fan of the book and I was a big fan of *The Lion, the Witch, and the Wardrobe*; it was similar in tone and scope to *Wrinkle*. I called him to ask if he would like to produce the film with me should Disney decide to move forward. He loved the idea, and negotiations began between Disney and Walden that lasted for eight months, but an agreement couldn't be reached. By 2009, Cary left Walden and convinced Dick Cook to make the film in New Zealand with a smaller budget, and Jeff Stockwell was hired to write the screenplay.

Over the years, I pretty much followed the three pieces of advice I had been given concerning the role of a producer: Be a pain in the ass; a producer just produces; and open a restaurant. I was a pain in the ass. Ask the Disney executives about emails and phone calls I placed regularly to check on the status of the project from 2005 to 2014, or the dozens of other executives I had worked with over the years trying to build a case for the project. However, out of respect for my mother, I tried to always be a lady while doing it. With respect to the comment "A producer produces," I just kept working every day trying to figure that one out. It continued to be a strange and unpredictable path. As for the third piece of advice—open a restaurant—I did better than that. I went to work for the Obama administration as a political appointee. The advice-giver had been right—it can take forever to get a movie made, and I had to do something else with my time. What I thought was a temporary detour while I waited for Disney to move ahead turned out to be the road I needed to take to reach my destination.

I came to discover that the word "government" means so much more than Congress that passes our laws, or the US Supreme Court that decides the constitutionality of those laws. The president of the United States heads up the executive branch and all the departments and agencies in that branch. I had spent my entire life around politics in one way or another and was familiar with the cabinet-level departments that were often in the news, including the departments of State, Defense, Treasury, and Justice. I was less familiar with the scope of work of the other departments or the 400 federal agencies and sub-agencies responsible for managing the third branch of government.

Once again through the kindness of a friend, I met with the director of the Office of Personnel Management (OPM) for a possible position in the new Obama administration. The federal government is often described as monotonous and bureaucratic, and as much as I needed a job, I worried that I might be entering a version of Central Central, the main city on Camazotz where everything and everyone is the same. I mentioned this in a very roundabout way with the director and he said, "Well, why don't you join our team and help us change that perception. President Obama promised to make working for the government 'cool again,' and we want to make good on that promise." I had thought it was almost a noble calling to work in government when I was a young girl since that is how my dad saw it. The director's offer to join their team was an offer that I couldn't refuse.

There are basically two ways to work in the government: as a political appointee or as a career employee. A political appointee is hired to represent the views of the administration in office, so my tenure would be connected to the time Obama held the office. A career employee is someone who works for different administrations and can stay in the government for decades. I was brought in to be the deputy director of communications as a Schedule C political appointee, and my role was to help amplify the workforce personnel policies for government employees to our many stakeholders: the public, other agencies, Congress, and the media. I joined a small team put together at OPM to find ways to help the public—and potential new recruits—see government as a cool place to work.

Our team held discussion groups across the various government agencies and found that working for the federal
government is cool. My experience showed me that the conventional perception of government as bureaucratic was
outdated and couldn't have been further from the truth. Dedi-
cated and committed people working to maintain the public
trust surrounded me. There were outliers, of course, but the
majority of the people I came in contact with took their job
very seriously. One leader at OPM described it to me in this
way: "I come to work every day to uphold the Constitution
of the United States." I was taken aback by the profundity of
that statement; not many people working in the private sector could say that. I found a way to produce—not movies, but
several dozen very successful three-minute videos that told
the federal employee story. We created a tag line for the video
series that best captured what we discovered about government workers: "They are our neighbors, our mothers, fathers,
sisters, brothers, aunts, and uncles—they are people like us."

It was fascinating to learn how much federal workforce
personnel policies, directly or indirectly, impact those working for state and local governments as well as the private
sector. This was especially true with respect to raising consciousness about equality in the workplace. While at OPM, the
initiative I found the most personally rewarding was helping
to amplify new thinking about diversity, which now incorporated the word "inclusion." The moniker "Equality and
Diversity," became "Equality, Diversity, and Inclusion."

To get a better handle on how best to communicate this
message within the agency and to a wider audience at large,

I volunteered to participate in a diversity and inclusion workshop. When I arrived at the first session, I was surprised how few government employees showed up. The reason for the awareness campaign was this very issue—too few people wanted to participate. As we sat around in a semicircle and started introducing ourselves, I found that not only were we a mix of different races and genders, but of generations, too, which brought more layers of differences. The word "inclusion" had been added to the slogan because the concept of inequality had evolved and a deeper dive was necessary to learn how to bridge the divide among us. Why was it so difficult for us to get along?

While participating in the workshop, I first heard the expression "unconscious biases"—beliefs that have been ingrained in us since childhood. These beliefs shape our behavior not just about race or gender, but our attitudes about an array of things including our views on politics and religion. I was unaware of my own biases and surprised to see how much had changed since I had been in a corporate setting. With four generations in the workforce, the unconscious biases we talked about were different from what I expected. Of course, race and gender were at the top of the list, but new biases had emerged based on age, where we had been raised, feelings about women in power, and our economic backgrounds. These discussions gave a whole new meaning to Madeleine's favorite line, "Like and equal area not the same thing at all." It was in this workshop that I finally really understood the meaning of that line. People don't need to be *alike* to be *equal*. The two words are entirely different and unrelated.

My newfound awareness had to do with a personal experience I had years earlier—except that I hadn't recognized it at the time as such. Every family has its daily rituals, and one of the most common ritual in any family with small children is picking up toys and clothes left scattered on the floor. I would often pick up Meg's baby shoes and leave them on the step to take downstairs on my next trip to her room. A week or so after Patrick died, I saw that the shoes stayed on the stairs longer than usual. I had never noticed that Patrick had taken the shoes downstairs as often as I did. Now, that may seem like a very small thing, but it was a huge revelation to me because I thought I did everything when it came to the kids.

I would often complain that he was not doing his fair share of household chores and he would just nod or shrug and say something along the lines that he would try to do better. I was so wrong. I measured his participation by my yardstick and not his. Patrick and I were co-parents and not alike at all when it came to getting things done around the house. I got upset with him because he wasn't like me. I had been so caught up in the meaning of inequality defined by how men treated women that I didn't see my own biases in how I viewed him. In that government workshop, a big wave of awakening washed over me.

Great conversations occurred within the group about the difference between like and equal. Women didn't want to become more *like* men to be *equal*, nor did people of color want to become more *like* whites; and the same was true for people who identified as LGBTQ, and between the different generations. The goal is not to be the same, but to be accepted and valued for who we are. This was the first step to establish a level playing field for everyone.

The generational differences really hit close to home for me. I needed to make more of an effort to learn from the millennial generation rather than becoming frustrated that they didn't see things from my generation's point of view—with my own kids as well as with my colleagues.

It had really burned me when I heard one of the millennials I worked with say his generation was the "innovation" generation. I asked "So, what about the people who invented the internet?" His biases towards my generation were just as stubborn as mine towards his. The solution? We discovered in the workshop the importance of finding the happy medium, although no one called it that. The words used were "respect for our differences"—to learn from one another rather than objectifying people just like the callers did on the radio call-in shows I produced years earlier. Seeing people as objects leads to wrong assumptions. Everything I had learned from Norman and Madeleine about making the impossible possible was achievable when we found those common bonds that bind us together. Norman used to say, "When you find yourself in a pile of manure, look around for the pony that must be hiding somewhere." I never fully appreciated the story until faced with how to find those common bonds. First, you have to believe that the pony exists—or in this case, that the common bonds exist.

The notion of like and equal not being the same thing played out rather unexpectedly in my journey to bring the movie to the screen. The very fact that my talents were different from the men I worked with was consistently seen as less than by others. I needed to partner with someone who had acquired experienced producing skills, but I brought equally important and different producing talents to the table that weren't always acknowledged as such.

An unconscious bias also existed in how men viewed Meg's journey of self-discovery in *Wrinkle*. In an interview, a writer whom I had never met said that the reason why *Wrinkle* was so difficult to adapt for the screen was because the story had no place to go once the father was rescued. I thought that guy (and it was a guy) didn't understand the story at all. The missing father is the MacGuffin—the trigger for the plot—but not the story. Once the father is rescued, the stakes are raised that much higher for Meg. It is because she is able to see the world differently than her father that she is able to find the only weapon against the dark force. The most fantastical element in the entire fantasy is that her father doesn't hold her back. With Mrs Whatsit's urging, he accepts that his daughter must return alone to the evil planet.

All three Mrs Ws know the only hope of rescuing Charles Wallace is for Meg to accept the task with grace and understanding, because Dr. Murry had failed when he tried to rescue his son. No executive ever believed a father would allow his daughter to return alone unless he was practically at death's door—the opposite of the point Madeleine had made. She had written about courage and bravery from a female point of view, and it was hard for men to accept her perspective. Inevitably, the studio executives would muse, "If the father can't go with her, how about Calvin?" It was so difficult for them to see that it was a game changer that both her father and friend *trusted in her to succeed* in a way they could not. The fact that Meg's father believed in her, that he accepted she could do something he couldn't do, elevated Meg and young girls everywhere to believe they, too, could be fighters.

Madeleine and I shared so much when it came to our fathers—men who in our eyes were larger than life and who influenced how we saw the world and ourselves. This journey for Madeleine, Meg, and me—and millions like us—was to learn how to stand on our own. Sadly, that also applied to my love and reliance on Madeleine as a mentor. There came the time when I had to let her go too. As the years passed, I could tell when we spoke on the phone that she was fading. Her granddaughter, Charlotte, likened it to speaking with someone on a cell phone that keeps breaking up due to a poor connection. In the summer of 2007, the inevitable came when Josephine, her oldest daughter, arranged for me to visit Madeleine in the nursing home where she was staying. She had her good days and bad ones, and Josephine warned me that Madeleine might not recognize me.

As we entered her room, I saw her sitting up in bed. She exclaimed with the same kind of joy I had always known, "Hello, Cathy!" I looked at Josephine and we both knew this might be the only thing she would say. I took the moment, knowing this was the last time I would ever see her and asked, "Why me, Madeleine? Why was I the one you trusted?" She replied, without missing a beat, "Because we are connected by an umbilical cord of love." I was the one who was at a loss for words.

With my daughter Caitlin and Madeleine at Crosswicks, 1997

In September, I attended her funeral near Crosswicks with my daughter Caitlin who had been one of Madeleine's many godchildren. As I listened to the music that day, I thought about the conversations we had over the years about the Mrs Ws. She was adamant that they were not women, but part of an energy force in the galaxies who took the shape of women for the sake of the children. I read somewhere that an energy force might have been present at creation in order to keep our galaxies in place and prevent them from spinning out of control. I believe that Madeleine is now connected to that force by an umbilical cord of love.

I felt like I had failed her. I hadn't found a way to bring the vision we shared to the big screen before she died. I also felt so alone. Tom, Patrick, Claire, and Madeleine were gone. Two years after Madeleine's funeral, my brother Chip died. There are no words to describe how much Chip meant to me. He had been my childhood playmate, my best buddy during my teen years and who was there for me after Patrick died. Chip always had a joke, a story about some nutty thing that he had done, or he would do his brilliant impersonation of the English actor Richard Burton that would inevitably get me to laugh. He had won the Frank Sinatra Award when he attended UCLA and went on to have success as a singer, songwriter, and voice teacher.

Chip had also struggled with depression his entire life. As with Tom, I thought if I loved Chip enough, I could help him overcome his challenges too. My brilliant, gorgeous, funny brother left this world on his own terms. It's still so difficult to write those words, but to honor Chip I must; it was his decision when he couldn't find a way to cope with his depression any longer. I can't imagine how hard it must have been for my parents to lose both their sons; it was devastating for me to lose both my brothers. Chip had written a song that we all loved called "Hug the Memories," and his wife, our family, and his friends continue to hug the memories.

Not too long after Chip died, I thought it was time to let the dream die. By 2011, the leadership at Disney had changed and so had their interest in *Wrinkle*. They passed on Jeff Stockwell's

My brother Chip Hand
PHOTO COURTESY OF ALDO PANZIERI

screenplay; my phone calls and emails went unanswered. There was something inside of me, however, that wouldn't let it go—there had to be a pony somewhere. I never forgot what Mr. Perenchio said about the need to have pants made of steel and be ready to take a nuclear bullet to get anything done in this town. I thought I had already done that, but maybe not. There is a definition of a hero that goes something like this: an ordinary person in an extraordinary situation who hangs on one minute longer. Not sure I would describe myself as a hero, but I'm glad I hung on one minute longer.

In 2013, fifty years after I first read *A Wrinkle in Time*, priorities changed at Disney again. Erin Westerman and Tendo Nagenda, two film executives at Disney, called to say they wanted me to meet with one of their top producers, Jim Whitaker. Jim had been a longtime fan of the book and wanted to explore the possibility of producing the film together. Not only was I happy to hear that Disney wanted to make the movie, but that workshop on diversity, equality, and inclusion helped me to appreciate and agree with the vision that would finally make my lifelong childhood dream come true.

11

Gathering of Allies

You've been trying for so long to
make the movie at an appointed time,
and it finally got made at the anointed time.

OPRAH WINFREY

I n April 2014, thirty-four years after meeting Madeleine L'Engle, I was on a plane to Los Angeles to meet Jim Whitaker, Jennifer Lee, and our Disney film executive, Tendo Nagenda. I reread the book for the umpteenth time on the flight, and this time I no longer identified just with Meg or Mrs. Murry but experienced the story through Mrs Whatsit's eyes. I imagined her sitting around a cosmic campfire somewhere in the universe with a bunch of rookie messengers, one of whom asks, "What is it that we do, exactly?" My imaginary Mrs Whatsit smiles and replies, "Let me tell you the story about a young girl named Meg Murry I once met on a dark and stormy night . . ."

Over three decades of effort came down to one word—a word Madeleine introduced me to in 1979—synchronicity.

According to Madeleine, *A Wrinkle in Time* was published exactly at the right time. If it had come out earlier or later, it might not have been successful. She believed that we had met exactly when we were supposed to meet to eventually make the movie. I believe that the movie got made when it was the right time for me to meet Sean Bailey, Tendo Nagenda, Jessica Virtue, Jim Whitaker, Jennifer Lee, and our visionary, Ava DuVernay.

The movie business had changed significantly since I first started my journey. Walt Disney's company had grown into the most powerful film studio in the world. It had acquired the libraries of Pixar, Marvel, and the biggest brand of all, Lucasfilm and the *Star Wars* franchise. The cost of films had skyrocketed, and streaming services made it harder and harder to get people to the movie theaters. In order for a project to receive a $100+ million budget, it was essential to have a well-established brand—and thankfully, *A Wrinkle in Time* was a well-known brand. In another extraordinary example of synchronicity, Alan Horn—the Alan Horn who approved my going after the rights in 1979—was now the chairman of Walt Disney Pictures. I couldn't believe my good fortune to have Alan in that position at this point in my, and the film's, journey. He had always been an important ally and someone I trusted completely.

I was filled with concern, worry, and trepidation when it came to starting anew. I was determined to do all I could to help navigate the possible pitfalls that lay ahead. Happily, my children were young adults and doing well on their own. The same month that the offices for *Wrinkle* opened, Meg graduated from MIT, Caitlin was living in New York and had a job she loved in the federal government, and Ben had moved to

With Alan Horn on set, February 2017
REPRODUCED BY PERMISSION FROM ALAN HORN

Los Angeles to pursue a career in the entertainment business. I could focus one hundred percent of my energies on my long-lost dream of producing *A Wrinkle in Time.*

From the moment I met Jim Whitaker, I was impressed with his quiet tenacity and keen interest in the development of the characters. He had started out as an intern at Imagine, a hugely successful production company founded by Ron Howard and Brian Glazer and worked his way up to become president of the company. Jim has an indispensable ability to make everything seem so doable. It's easy to be overwhelmed with the totality that goes into getting a top team in place to the satisfaction of the studio. He simply said, "We just have to hit our mark. Then we identify and aim for the next mark."

Much had changed since 1980 when there were no female writers to hire for a big budget film. Jennifer Lee had written and co-directed Disney's mega hit *Frozen* based on the Hans Christian Andersen classic *Snow Queen*. The film went on to earn more than $1.3 billion worldwide at the box office and would win the Academy Award for Best Picture for Animation. Jenn's exceptional ability to bring a modern perspective to that classic tale without losing any of its beauty and scope was the intangible quality to make *Wrinkle* work that I had been seeking for decades. We heard that she had been an

With Jennifer Lee on set during production, 2016
REPRODUCED BY PERMISSION FROM JENNIFER LEE

ardent fan of the book since she was nine years old and asked to meet with Jim and me. My worries completely vanished the moment I met her in person. I felt as if I was in the presence of a young Madeleine L'Engle because Jenn radiated such joy. A surprising bonus was to learn she had studied physics and not only loved the science in the book but understood it in a way I never did. When this brilliant, funny, compassionate, and accomplished woman signed on to work with us, our lives forever changed.

Jennifer, Jim, and I met with Tendo to hear Jenn's take on the material. We couldn't have asked for a stronger ally and film executive than Tendo. He grew up in Los Angeles with a father from Uganda and a mother from Belize, which afforded him a childhood of typical American experiences mixed with an international perspective. Tendo had worked on several Disney movies, including *Saving Mr. Banks*, before we started working together. I was delighted to learn that he had been the executive on that film, because Walt Disney's experience working with P. L. Travers on the adaptation of *Mary Poppins* wasn't too dissimilar from my early experiences working with Madeleine. I thought it was one more example of synchronicity. Tendo's experience bringing that film to life gave him a better understanding than most of the struggles to find the perfect blend of book and film based on a childhood classic. It was essential to get Tendo fully committed to the project because he was the film's chief advocate within the studio hierarchy. Jennifer wowed him with her vision of a big, beautiful story told against a cosmic backdrop about a young girl's quest to rescue her father.

Finally, I had the right studio executive in place, the perfect producing partner, and we couldn't have hoped for a better screenwriter. In August 2014, Walt Disney Pictures announced that Jennifer had been hired to write the screenplay for *A Wrinkle in Time*, and the internet exploded with the news. In the short span of twenty-four hours, the announcement was carried on all the major news outlets in the United States and around the world. I read headlines in Spanish, German, Italian, and Japanese and thought how surreal it all felt. It was thrilling and yet bittersweet because I was unable to share the moment with Madeleine. I missed my mentor and friend, but I had developed a strong bond with her granddaughter Charlotte Jones Voiklis. We shared an understanding of the book, and her friendship would prove invaluable throughout the time I worked on the movie.

The first big hurdle was the screenplay. I'll never forget the call Jim and I had with Jennifer after we read her draft. It was just the three of us on the phone and our big question was, "Is there a movie here?" The answer was unanimously "Yes!" Jim thought it had all the elements we would need for a film, I thought she had captured the essence of the book, and Jennifer seemed to enjoy our collaboration. The call couldn't have been better. We just had a few notes for the draft that would be sent to the studio for their review. Tendo read it and agreed that the film was there, and Jim called me to say, "We hit our first mark."

We immediately began making our wish list for directors. Early on, we shared the thought that since this movie is a classic heroine's journey, wouldn't it be great if a woman could direct it. But who? Although the list of potential candidates was extremely limited, I was thankful there was even a small list of female directors to consider. In November 2015, I read Maureen Dowd's *NY Times Magazine* article, "The Women of Hollywood Speak Out." Dowd had interviewed 100 women in the entertainment business about their views concerning the ongoing sexism in Hollywood. One of the biggest issues they faced, according to the article, was how difficult it was for a promising new female director to make the leap to a big budget feature.

Jennifer had been interviewed for the article, so I called her to discuss it. Dowd's piece cited some pretty sobering figures: "In both 2013 and 2014, women were only 1.9 percent of the directors for the 100 top-grossing films. Excluding their art-house divisions, the six major studios released only three movies last year with a female director." We felt very strongly that *Wrinkle* was the perfect vehicle to give this hard-to-come-by opportunity to a female director.

The irony is that Dowd failed to mention the one woman who had directed a film in 2014 that went on to be nominated for Best Picture at the 2015 Academy Awards—Ava DuVernay. Ava had a history of being "the first" throughout her career. She was the first female director of color to win the directing award at the Sundance Film Festival, the first female director of color to be nominated for a Golden Globe, and the first female director of color to have directed a film nominated for Best Picture by the Academy of Motion Pictures Arts and Sciences.

Ava didn't follow the conventional path to directing. She had been a well-regarded publicist who had used her own funds to make a short film. That short led to her first full-length feature made for only $50,000. She won the Director's Award at Sundance for her second feature, *The Middle of Nowhere*. Then, in 2014, she directed *Selma*, based on Martin Luther King, Jr.'s fight for voting rights, which was nominated for Best Picture in 2015. Ava was at the top of all our lists. Tendo was looking for the right project for her at Disney and gave her our script. Ava had never read the book as a child, but it was a favorite of both her sister and her agent. After she read the screenplay, we got the call that she wanted to meet.

In January 2016, the president of Walt Disney Pictures, Sean Bailey, convened a meeting in his office with Ava, Jennifer, Tendo, their colleague Jessica Virtue, Jim, and me. It was my first meeting with Sean, and I was captivated by everything he hoped to achieve with *Wrinkle*. He wanted us to be bold in our undertaking and to achieve all our hopes and dreams for the project. Ava was like no one I had ever met. She has such compelling energy and intelligence; I listened intently to everything she said. She asked all the right questions, seemed genuinely interested in the project, and wanted to make the film more urban with a diverse cast. I wasn't sure what that meant or how it would translate to screen, but it seemed like a new and exciting way to bring a book written in 1963 into the twenty-first century.

I thought hiring Ava was a done deal, but while standing in a foot of snow campaigning for Hillary Clinton in New Hampshire, I learned that Colin Trevorrow and Derek Connolly (*Jurassic World*) wanted Ava to direct their film, *Intelligent Life*, for Amblin Entertainment. We felt that Ava was worth fighting for; she had impressed us all with her

Outside Disney executive office, May 2016

creativity and enthusiasm for the chance to create the different worlds the characters visit on their adventure. Sean kicked into high gear, and with Tendo and others at the studio, did whatever it took to convince her to direct *Wrinkle*. To this day, I don't know all the back and forth that occurred, but their efforts paid off and I was extremely grateful.

While Jim, his associate Adam Borba, and I worked with Jenn and Ava on script revisions, we also started the rigorous job of pulling together the key department heads in close consultation with the studio. Temporary offices were set up in a building close to the studio, and one of the best executive producers in the business, Doug Merrifield, joined our team and immediately set about developing a budget. The next big step was for Ava to lead the creation of a look and feel for the film and to get studio sign off on the plan. We brought together A-list talent to work with her to visualize the film, aware that the studio could pull the plug at any moment.

In May 2016, a crucial meeting was held for Ava to present the storyboards to the top leaders at Walt Disney Pictures. When the meeting started, I had the same out-of-body experience I had riding up that elevator with Madeleine in 1979—now with the end goal in sight. The artwork was stunning; everyone was impressed with Ava's vision. The consensus was that the film looked like nothing they had seen before, and we were given the go ahead to begin assembling the cast. We had hit our mark.

In June, the office for Tesseract Productions officially opened and many more production personnel were hired. The search was on for the three children, the Mrs Ws, Dr. and Mrs. Murry,

With Ava DuVernay and Oprah Winfrey on a hilltop in New Zealand.
We landed gloriously on Uriel!

REPRODUCED BY PERMISSION FROM AVA DUVERNAY AND FROM HARPO, INC.

the Happy Medium, and the Man with the Red Eyes, as well as the supporting characters. Ava hoped to find three iconic actresses to play the three Mrs Ws. She and Oprah were great friends; the story goes that once Oprah heard we were scheduled to shoot in New Zealand, she asked Ava if she could come along. Ava then gave her the script to read and Oprah fell in love with Mrs Which.

Reese Witherspoon was not just an Academy Award-winning actress but one of the most successful producers in town. She had been a huge fan of *Wrinkle* since childhood, had read all the books in the series, and loved the idea of playing Mrs Whatsit.

Mindy Kaling is a powerhouse, too, and had been a huge fan of science fiction/fantasy movies, but never saw a character who looked like her. She was happy to change that for a new generation of filmgoers and was cast as Mrs Who.

Finding the children was not quite as easy due to the ages called for in the story. Our casting director, Aisha Coley, watched hundreds of audition tapes. "I'll know it when I see it," applied to our search for the actress to play Meg. We had many conversations about possible young actresses for the role, and they all ended with the question, "Have you seen the tape of Storm Reid?" The actress chosen to play Meg Murry would have to carry the entire film, and we all thought Storm was up to the task. The only hiccup was that she had another commitment that had to be addressed before we could hire her.

Once Storm got the part, we brought her in to read opposite the various young boys we considered for Calvin and Charles Wallace. Aisha conducted a worldwide search to find the actor to play Charles Wallace and discovered Deric McCabe who lived ten minutes from the studio in Burbank, California. Finding the right Calvin turned out to be the most difficult. Like Meg, he, too, was in that "in between" awkward time in life. Levi Miller lives in Australia, and after seeing his audition tape, we brought him to California to test with Storm. Levi looked the part and he came across as empathetic, which is the essence of Calvin.

There is so much that goes into the calculation for the right actor for any role—the studio has criteria to meet and the hope is those interests coincide with the director's vision. We all agreed we had to have an actor with real star power to play Dr. Murry because the impetus for the story rests on finding the missing father. Both the studio and Ava were excited about the possibility of working with Chris Pine. We were lucky that Jim had worked with Chris on another film and was able to persuade him to meet with Ava. I think it took just one meeting for her to convince him to take the role. As for Meg's mother, we needed someone who was strong, intelligent, loving, and had a good chemistry with Chris. We hired Gugu Mbatha-Raw as soon as she said yes.

In *Wrinkle*, the Happy Medium is a woman, but we changed her to a man to bring some male/female humor with the Mrs Ws. We were looking for someone who can find both the humor and poignancy in any scene; Zach Galifinakis has that wide range as an actor. Michael Pena has an equally broad range, and we wanted an actor who could seem genuinely friendly, but with a sense of menace just under the surface to play the Man with the Red Eyes.

By early September 2016, we were in pre-production mode and I moved full time to Los Angeles. Our daily production meetings around the conference table grew larger each day. I think we were all a little surprised by how much interest the project was generating in the press. The selection of Ava as the first woman of color to direct a big budget film *was* newsworthy. The studio's decision to have a diverse cast reflected their interest—and Ava's—in making films for an increasingly diverse audience. It is a tribute to Ava that she used her position to hire as many women, and women and men of color, as possible.

After everyone was cast and the initial high subsided, the enormity of what we were doing hit me like a ton of bricks. This was no longer the childhood dream that I carried around in my head for decades—this was a massive undertaking with hundreds of people and a studio willing to invest a huge amount of money. I tried to convince myself that I had simply tessered—traveled in the fifth dimension—from my lunch with Madeleine at Windows on the World to that first meeting with Ava in Sean's office, but of course that wasn't the case. If the time spent on this endeavor were only measured in *Kairos* time, then it did seem like a few minutes had passed since I worked with Norman, met Madeleine, and the Miramax version aired. In reality, it had been almost forty years in *Chronos* time by the time production began.

I was reluctant to admit to myself how much had evolved since I had begun my journey and that the story needed to be updated. When I first met Madeleine, it had been only seventeen years since the book was published. Societal norms hadn't progressed that much between 1962 and 1979. Even though Madeleine had been thirty-four years older than I, we were on the same wavelength in our conversations about life and the adaptation of *Wrinkle*. We had spoken about the need to collapse events or to create a few additional scenes, like meeting Meg's father before he disappears, but nothing about the characters or themes. It had been the same dynamic with Norman; despite a thirty-year age difference, it never seemed to be a problem.

He surrounded himself with younger people, and the staff writers on his shows were a mix of veteran writers who had decades of experience and new and upcoming writers. The blending of ages behind the camera as well as in front on *All in the Family* and his other TV series assured their appeal to a wide audience.

When Sean and Ava spoke about taking *Wrinkle* into the twenty-first century, I didn't fully grasp that that meant letting go of some of the things I loved about the book that belonged in the twentieth century. I had been so focused on getting the film made, I was oblivious to the huge paradigm shift that had occurred in the intervening years and how it would affect the movie. With the arrival of the internet, the cell phone, and so many other technological advancements, the way we did business, lived our lives, and related to one another had been transformed.

The author Studs Turkle once made a comment to Norman and me during the early days of People For the American Way about the impact of the nightly news. He had said history changes at six every night when the nightly news airs, and it hadn't been like that before the invention of radio and television, when it could have taken days, weeks, or even months before people heard about new developments. In the twenty-first century, new developments are available every second. This paradigm shift required that we take a fresh look at the characters and themes in *Wrinkle* for today's audience. There was a smaller age difference between Ava, Jennifer, Jim, and me than there had been with Madeleine and Norman, but I discovered the challenge I had in working with the film team was generational.

The hardest truth for me to accept throughout the entire process—from script development to the final film—was that the passage of chronological time meant I had to let go of my interpretation of the book to support Ava's vision. Jennifer and Ava helped me understand how necessary it was to bring new language and perspective to the story. The character arcs that once resonated earlier didn't seem as relevant; mainly because young girls' self-esteem had improved over the years. I had always loved the old-fashioned charm of setting *Wrinkle* in a small New England village, the perfect set up for a mystery, but Ava wanted an urban setting that would be more relatable to today's audience. For some reason, the Brits can still get away with magical things happening in small villages, but it's tough to pull off in the US. Then there was the troublesome issue that many memorable moments in the book had already been used in other movies by the time we were ready to make ours.

When I saw Marvel's movie *Captain America: The First Avenger*, I was shocked to discover the tesseract was an important plot device in the story, though it was used slightly differently than in *Wrinkle*. I didn't remember whether Madeleine had said where she saw the word, but she never mentioned Marvel comic books. After a little digging, I discovered that the science fiction writer Charles Howard Hinton first used "tesseract" in 1880 in his article "What Is the Fourth Dimension?" Hinton's son Sebastian invented the jungle gym that has become ubiquitous on every playground based on a model his father used to teach his children about three dimensions.

Madeleine may have read about Hinton's tesseract and created a way for three otherworldly creatures to travel in the fifth dimension. This transformation from what was meant in one era to becoming something completely different in a new one was exactly what Ava faced in re-imagining the tesseract, the look and feel of the various planets, the evil force in the universe, and the characterizations of Mrs Whatsit, Who, and Which. The dilemma we faced was how to bring the characters and themes forward without losing all that endeared them to millions of people for over fifty years?

Was it fair to those first in line to buy tickets to see the movie version of their favorite childhood book and not include some favorite words, descriptions of a scene, or a character that would fulfill their expectations? It is laughable that anyone would think of me as the book police—I was trying hard to support Ava's vision as well as those of the readers I had met over the years. The clause in the original contract about not changing characters and themes had been dropped somewhere along the line in negotiations either with Miramax or Disney. Still, everyone wanted to stay as true as possible to the original intent of the story, which as always was up for interpretation.

The first big question we wrestled with was the right tone for the film. There was considerable back and forth about whether it should be like *Star Wars* or *The Wizard of Oz*. The consensus was that *A Wrinkle in Time* had far more in common with *The Wizard of Oz* than *Star Wars*, and the tone needed to be more in line with a great fantasy adventure rather than a science fiction action picture. The challenge became to recognize every beat, character trait, and plot point of the book and to push through them into something new for the film. There even was

a moment when I had to fight back—once again—the suggestion that Calvin return with Meg to save her brother, but this
time when I explained why Meg had to return alone, the idea
was quickly dropped. Things had changed for the better.

If so much had to be reworked, why even make the movie?
What was the compelling argument for this timeless tale of
love and courage to be made now? The answer is in what Jean
Houston, one of the co-founders of the Human Potential Movement, said when I met her years earlier. "Since *A Wrinkle in
Time*'s existence, it has virtually taken on the status of a world
story, of a world myth. We are becoming citizens in a universe
larger than our aspirations, more complex than all our dreams.
People are reaching out with love across the cosmos embracing
different forms and possibilities. We are being called upon to
really redefine the human condition and children are critical
to this." Ava was determined to bring that message to young people who identified with her experiences growing up in Compton,
California, which were very different than mine growing up in
Austin, Texas, Washington, DC, or West Los Angeles.

In the 1980s, when Ava was a young girl living in Compton,
the city had the highest crime rate in the state of California.
Chances are there weren't many well-stocked elementary
school libraries back then in Compton. While the line "like
and equal are not the same thing" ultimately ended up on the
cutting room floor, the use of a diverse cast set in an urban
area was the embodiment of its spirit. Ava's vision gave young
people of color the opportunity to see themselves as citizens in
a universe larger than our aspirations, more complex than all
our dreams.

Oprah turned to me one day and said, "You've been trying for so long to make the movie at an appointed time, and it finally got made at the anointed time." She was right in more ways than one. While Ava's new way of looking at childhood was groundbreaking, there were other forces emerging in the world that made *Wrinkle* as timely as ever. Madeleine always believed that Meg's inner struggles mirrored the macro struggle between light and dark in the world around her. The voices of division replacing those of reason and unity in the 1950s during the rise of McCarthyism, or in the 1980s with the message of religious intolerance that depended on a specific political point of view, were present again in 2016.

The evil force on Camazotz uses the Man with the Red Eyes to create a climate of fear and division. He tries to seduce Meg into thinking only he can solve her problems, but she knows that is a lie. We honored one of Madeleine's greatest themes, to show that we don't have to become like the fearful, conforming people on Camazotz. We have free will and we may make other choices. This was what Meg did, and she triumphs in the end. She becomes a warrior against such darkness.

As a result of the political climate at the time of the filming, there was one significant shift that impacted a layer of the story—the Christian references. The topic had been written about and I'd had dozens of conversations with people who experience the book as a Christian story, but the politicization of Christianity we saw emerging in the 1980s has only grown over the decades. Any specific reference to Christianity could be interpreted as a political statement. We worked to find a happy medium—a way to bridge the core theme of faith that is central to the story and make it accessible to people of all religions or of no religion at all. We relied on the words Madeleine shared years earlier as our guiding philosophy: "To write a story, to paint a picture, to compose a sonata or a symphony is a religious activity, because it is an act of creation!"

On November 2, 2016, we hit our mark. Principle photography began in downtown Los Angeles, and it was almost otherworldly to hear: "Picture is up! Here we go! Rolling! Sound speed! Still rolling! Ready? Here we go and action!"

With Jim Whitaker and Adam Borba on the first day
of principal photography, November 2016

REPRODUCED BY PERMISSION FROM JIM WHITAKER AND ADAM BORBA

12

Tesser Well

Tesser well and may you land gloriously on Uriel.

MADELEINE L'ENGLE

One of the great things about working on a film is the downtime between setups when you get to have conversations with individual cast and crewmembers. Everyone has such a unique story about how they arrived; there is no single yellow brick road to follow for a career in the entertainment business—there are tens of thousands. A typical way to enter the business is through a relative, or the friend of a friend who makes an introduction to someone who introduces you to someone else. Of course, attending film school, apprenticing with a pro, and pure luck also count. No matter how our cast and crew arrived to our set, they all had one thing in common—they were excellent at what they did.

As I observed Ava on location scouts, leading production meetings, standing by the storyboard discussing the next shot, or working with the actors, I knew I was in the presence of excellence. I felt the same watching Jim Whitaker, executive producers Adam Borba and Doug Merrifield, director of photography Tobias Schliessler, visual effects supervisor Rich McBride, costume designer Paco Delgado, production designer Naomi Shohan, and all their teams. Everyone was excellent at what they did and worked hard every day to bring a beautiful film "to a theater near you."

What I had learned in that workshop on inclusion when working for the federal government served as a roadmap of sorts in the making of *Wrinkle*. There were lots of opinions—that is what collaboration is all about, and we all have unconscious biases of one sort or another. I had to constantly let go of old ideas and welcome the new. We were there to support Ava who was open to suggestions and recommendations throughout the entire process. I learned that the role of a producer is to know how to climb out of holes—not to keep digging. My inner mantra was something Jennifer Lee wrote for Mrs Which who says to Meg: "Don't you realize the trillions of events that had to occur since the birth of our universe to lead to the making of you exactly as you are?" I certainly knew the trillions of events that had occurred for us to make *A Wrinkle in Time*.

Typically, no one is allowed near the DP (director of photography) when filming, but Tobias often invited me to watch from his tent. I think he surmised better than most what it meant to me to see the scenes come alive. There were so many moments that brought back years of memories. As I watched the crew set up the cameras and lights in the

Murry kitchen, I could hear Madeleine say, "I was never a very good housekeeper." When I saw the piano in the living room, I remembered Madeleine telling me that she played Bach whenever she got stuck in her writing. As I watched the filming of the iconic ant and string, I thought of Madeleine holding her skirt tightly with her hands demonstrating what she meant when she wrote that a straight line is not the shortest distance between two points. The set decorator asked for family photos from the cast and crew to dress the house. I gave her a copy of the unfinished portrait Henriette Wyeth painted of me the week I met Madeleine and the painting made it into the movie.

The night before we were to film the backyard sequence when the children tesser for the first time, we went on a tech scout to block the scene. Jim, Ava, and I, along with the assistant director, director of photography, and others, met to discuss the set ups for the following day. There wasn't a cloud in the sky and I was transported back to the first time Madeleine asked me to take a walk across the field behind Crosswicks to the creek where she liked to sit and think. As I listened to the conversations going on around me, I felt the cool autumn breeze of that October day and thought how lucky I was to have had the opportunity to just listen to her. It was bittersweet for me to watch Ava and Oprah together because their relationship reminded me of mine with Madeleine and how much I wished she were still alive to enjoy this moment.

Someone asked me to name my favorite planet in the story. I answered with Mrs Whatsit's line: "Uriel is my favorite planet in the universe, no offense to Earth." It was breathtaking to see Hawea Lake in South Island, New Zealand, which would become creature Whatsit's view as she soared high above Uriel with the children on her back. The other beautiful experience working in New Zealand was looking up at the night sky. The stars there are brighter than anyplace I had ever been and seemed so close it was almost like I could reach up and touch them. No matter what hemisphere, looking up at the stars always elicits the question Madeleine asked when she sat by the dying embers of the campfire over which she had cooked dinner and wondered: What is out there?

When we were back in Southern California, the Santa Ana winds appeared as if on cue during the last week of production. These were the same fierce winds that blew through my window when I first read A Wrinkle in Time and now tossed the trees as I drove up the hill to the Santa Clarita sound stage just outside of Los Angeles. I exited my car, walked over to the edge of the parking lot, and stared at the neighborhoods below. Feeling the wind whip through my hair, I thought about what Jean Houston said: A Wrinkle in Time was made when we were ready for it to be made.

Once production came to an end, the arduous task of integrating the visual effects and editing the film began. Months were spent in the editing room with ongoing conversations among the studio executives, Ava, and other members on the team. I was sorely disappointed when the character of Aunt Beast and the action that takes place on her planet, Ixchel, had to be cut. We had filmed the scene with the best of intentions, but once we got in the editing room, it just didn't work. The biggest problem was that the character as described in the book didn't translate well to the screen, and no matter what we tried we just couldn't make her believable. We held onto the scene as long as we could, but when the focus group responses reflected what we knew to be true, we had to let the character and scene go.

Posing for photos on the red carpet, February 26, 2018

Times Square in New York City, March 2018

There were other wins that offset that loss. Ava was a big fan of the singer-songwriter Sade and hoped to convince her to write a special song for *Wrinkle*. Even though Sade had been on hiatus from songwriting for several years, Ava succeeded in persuading her to return to the recording studio. Sade's haunting song "Flower of the Universe" beautifully captured Meg's journey.

On February 26, 2018, the premiere took place at the El Capitan Theater in Hollywood. It was one of the happiest moments in my life. My children were there, my younger sister Bridget, and several close girlfriends. Before the film began, Ava walked out on the stage to thank everyone for coming and introduced the cast, Jennifer, Jim, and me. As I walked out on stage and heard Ava say, "One of our producers, Catherine Hand, who dreamt of making this since she was a young girl," I had one last out-of-body experience and thought, "We did it!"

A week later, I spent opening weekend in New York visiting several movie theaters in different parts of town to watch audience reactions. No matter the location—in Harlem, the Upper West Side, or the East Village—the expression on the faces of young girls in the audience was everything. They could see themselves on the screen and feel what it was like to become the heroine of the story. I spoke to a few families at each theater and young girls were so excited to meet someone who helped bring the movie to the screen. One of my goals had been to get this story to a wider audience, and one month after the release of the film, the book ranked number one on the USA Today's Best-Selling Books List and over one million copies were sold within weeks.

Of all the comments made about the film, one carried the most weight with me. The Academy Award-winning actress Brie Larson (*Room*, *Captain Marvel*) had the courage to say, "I don't need a forty-year-old white dude to tell me what didn't work about *A Wrinkle in Time*. It wasn't made for him! I want to know what it meant to women of color, biracial women, to teen women of color." She was articulating the truth that there are still so many hard-to-overcome unconscious biases in how films are made, experienced, and reviewed. Oprah said it best: "This film will have an impact long after its release in ways we can't even begin to imagine." The goal wasn't just about box office success; it was about giving others a chance to create a new narrative for their generation. Ava's vision matters. Something else mattered, too: watching the Walt Disney logo come up on a big screen. It was such a meaningful connection to the promise I made to myself so long ago.

After the hoopla died down and I returned to my life in Washington, DC, I fell into a deep depression. I felt so much loss. My lifetime journey was over and I wasn't sure what was next. The film didn't do as well as we had hoped, and I wasn't going to get the call about sequels. *A Wrinkle in Time* is the first book in a trilogy. If it had been a financial success, there was a good chance that the studio would have been interested in adapting the other books. Unfortunately, we didn't hit the numbers needed at the box office for that to happen, but my sense of loss was about more than the end of a journey. I was feeling the loss I still carried for my late husband, my two brothers, Madeleine, and others I had loved and lost along the way. Somehow in my mind, as long as I was actively trying to get the movie made I was still connected to them all, if ever so tangentially. Now I had to let go of all those I loved who had died too.

As a way to work through my depression, I decided it was time to finally face why I stayed so committed to bring *A Wrinkle in Time* to the screen. I thought that if I could answer that "why," then I would find my next great adventure. I had jotted down notes over the years, written a chapter or two here and there, but could never see how best to chronicle something that took fifty years to accomplish. Then I joined a small writers' group and decided to tell them my story. It was as if I was Mrs Whatsit sitting at that campfire telling the story about what happened after I read a book called *A Wrinkle in Time* on a dark and windy night.

In writing this book I found the "why" that was expressed best in a speech Teddy Roosevelt gave over a hundred years ago. That speech inspired a very young congressman named Lyndon Johnson who passed along his admiration for Roosevelt's words to my father, who in turn passed it along to me. Roosevelt said:

It is not the critic who counts; not the man who points
out how the strong man stumbles, or where the doer
of deeds could have done them better. The credit
belongs to the man who is actually in the arena, whose
face is marred by dust and sweat and blood; who
strives valiantly; who errs, who comes up short

again and again, because there is no effort without
error and shortcoming; but who does actually strive to
do the deeds; who knows great enthusiasms, the great
devotions; who spends himself in a worthy cause;
who at the best knows in the end the triumph of high
achievement, and who at the worst, if he fails, at least
fails while daring greatly, so that his place shall never
be with those cold and timid souls who neither know
victory nor defeat.

I dared greatly to make the impossible possible and the
effort was worth the unexpected challenges and the considerable heartache. I had been away from the day-to-day
activities of the entertainment business for thirty years
before the film was made; anyone would think it impossible to get a movie produced under those circumstances. My
quest to bring A Wrinkle in Time to the screen has been like
a gust of wind—an unexpected force of nature that scattered
everything in new directions.

My journey afforded me an opportunity to get into the arena;
the great byproduct of my efforts was everything I had learned
in the struggles and the fight to get it made. In convincing others about the merit of the project I internalized all that the
book offers to people at different times in their lives: the joy I
felt as a young girl when I first read the book; the inspiration I
experienced when I first met Madeleine and was introduced to
the story through her eyes; the importance the book held when
I worked alongside Norman in his efforts to counter the religious right. I learned to have faith when I doubted my abilities

and to remember it's how we use our talents that count. In the act of making good on my childhood promise, I found the courage to face down the grief of my husband's death.

Madeleine gave me an autographed copy of *A Wrinkle in Time* and signed it with "Tesser well and may you land gloriously on Uriel." I remember asking myself at the time what she meant by "tesser well." I have come to understand that tesser well is an encouragement to get in the arena—and learn how to become a warrior against the darkness. We often use the word *warrior* to define those who pick up arms to defend our country at a time of war, but there are other kinds of warriors. It takes courage to fight on the battlefield, and it takes another kind of courage to find those common bonds that illuminate the human spirit. Whether they are on the battlefield or on the home front, a warrior doesn't fight only for him or herself, but for something greater than self, and I found the need to keep the darkness at bay only deepens over time.

Upon my return to Washington, DC, I kept a promise to my father that I would interview him for his memoir. I discovered that all his mysterious business trips were moments spent bringing people together to make the world a better place. His stories about meeting Pope Paul VI, attending Winston Churchill's funeral, traveling to the Paris Air Show with Vice President Humphrey, and so many other remarkable moments influenced my desire to see the bigger picture. My mother, too, who accompanied him on many of those trips, has spent thirty years designing beautiful jewelry to honor and celebrate her love of America. One of her most famous pieces is a small American flag engraved with the words "One

Walt Disney's office, May 22, 2018

Country One Destiny." Those words were embroidered in the coat Abraham Lincoln wore the night he was assassinated. I love that pin; it's a reminder that we truly are in this together and we have to find those common bonds—they do exist. I never understood before, but I had a head start in life becoming a warrior because I was raised by warriors, even if there were plenty of times when I felt inadequate and unqualified.

As Madeleine said, inadequate, unqualified people have done important things because they knew they could do it. But where does that feeling of knowing they could do it come from?

I have learned that it comes from finding a love for someone or something that gives you the courage to do what needs to be done to find your way home. Madeleine said it best: "Love isn't what you feel, it's what you do." For me, the tesseract is a metaphor for the connection we all have to that energy force— love—that keeps our galaxies in place and prevents them from spinning out of control. I loved my children so fiercely I was able to get us through our darkest days. I loved *Wrinkle* so fiercely I was able to hang on one minute longer. I spent over fifty years bringing a story to the screen about a young, insecure girl searching for her place in the world, not knowing that my effort would help me find my way home.

As I sit here writing these last few sentences with my little dog, Cody, by my side, I just have one question that may never be answered. Do you think that librarian who first gave me a copy of *A Wrinkle in Time* was actually Mrs Whatsit in disguise? If so, may she knock on your door, too, on a dark and stormy— or windy—night.

Acknowledgements

There are no words to adequately thank all the people I have met along my journey. You know who you are. Thank you. This book would never have happened without the support and encouragement of my writers' group, the team at Bold Story Press and my family and close friends. Aviva Kempner, Catherine Wyler, Annie Groer, Jennifer Lawson, Judy Hallet, and Phylis Geller, thank you for getting together once a month to share your writing and read mine. I owe a debt of gratitude to Jadi Waldron, Nancy Radin, Maureen Foster, Charlotte Jones Voiklis, Rita Cahill, and Ruth Golden, who believed I had a story worth telling no matter how long it took. A big thank you to Emily Barrosse and her team at Bold Story Press. I admire Emily's goal to publish bold stories by and for women and grateful she had faith in mine. I want to especially thank Karen Gulliver for her helpful edits, Julianna Scott Fein for keeping us on track, and Karen Polaski for such a beautiful cover.

This book wouldn't have been possible without my great friend and collaborator Susan Slonaker. She knew my story better than I did, and I am profoundly grateful for her invaluable input. Then there is my oldest daughter, Caitlin, who was the best sounding board, cheerleader, and tough taskmaster any writer or mother could hope for. Thank you, Susan and Cat, for all you did to bring this book to fruition. To everyone else who read multiple versions and gave me helpful feedback, thank you from the bottom of my heart.

About Bold Story Press

B old Story Press is a curated, woman-owned hybrid publishing company with a mission of publishing well-written stories by women. If your book is chosen for publication, our team of expert editors and designers will work with you to publish a professionally edited and designed book. Every woman has a story to tell. If you have written yours and want to explore publishing with Bold Story Press, contact us at https://boldstorypress.com.

BOLD STORY PRESS

The Bold Story Press logo, designed by Grace Arsenault, was inspired by the nom de plume, or pen name, a sad necessity at one time for female authors who wanted to publish. The woman's face hidden in the quill is the profile of Virginia Woolf, who, in addition to being an early feminist writer, founded and ran her own publishing company, Hogarth Press.

Made in the USA
Columbia, SC
02 December 2022

72287283R00171